An Insider's Guide to
Building a Successful
Consulting Practice

An Insider's Guide to
Building a Successful
Consulting Practice

Bruce L. Katcher with Adam Snyder

AMACOM

American Management Association

New York • Atlanta • Brussels • Chicago • Mexico City • San Francisco
Shanghai • Tokyo • Toronto • Washington, D. C.

Special discounts on bulk quantities of AMACOM books are available to corporations, professional associations, and other organizations. For details, contact Special Sales Department, AMACOM, a division of American Management Association, 1601 Broadway, New York, NY 10019.

Tel: 800-250-5308   Fax: 518-891-2372
Email: specialsls@amanet.org
Website: www.amacombooks.org/go/specialsales
To view all AMACOM titles go to: www.amacombooks.org

This publication is designed to provide accurate and authoritative information in regard to the subject matter covered. It is sold with the understanding that the publisher is not engaged in rendering legal, accounting, or other professional service. If legal advice or other expert assistance is required, the services of a competent professional person should be sought.

Library of Congress Cataloging-in-Publication Data

Katcher, Bruce Leslie, 1953-
  An insider's guide to building a successful consulting practice / Bruce L. Katcher with Adam Snyder. —1st ed.
      p. cm.
  Includes index.
  ISBN-13: 978-0-8144-1436-1
  ISBN-10: 0-8144-1436-2
  1. Business consultants. 2. Consultants. 3. Consulting firms—Management. 4. New business enterprises—Management. 5. Success in business. I. Snyder, Adam. II. Title.
  HG69.C6.K38 2010
  001--dc22

                                                                2009033306

Printing number

10 9

Contents

Introduction

A T APPROXIMATELY **2:00 PM** on Thursday, February 18, 1993, I was sitting in my Wellesley Hills, Massachusetts, office at a large international consulting firm. My new boss came into my office and said, "Bruce, we are going to have to lay you off." I was devastated. Immediately, my mind started racing. How was I going to support my family? How much severance would I receive? How soon would I have to leave? Should I look for work at another consulting firm, or a corporate job, or go back to teaching college?

I was anxious, scared, and angry. I felt powerless. What happened next changed my life. A lightbulb went on in my mind. "I am not going to let this ever happen to me again," I said to myself. "Nobody is ever going to have total control over my financial fate again. I am going into business for myself so that I can control my own destiny."

The experience reminded me of that famous scene from the classic movie, *Gone with the Wind*, when Scarlett O'Hara returns at the end of the Civil War to Tara, the magnificent Southern plantation where she was raised. She finds that her home had been used as a military headquarters. All of the artwork and furniture are gone. The slaves, of course, have left. Her father has gone mad. She is devastated. She doesn't know what to do. She's hungry, but there's no food in the house. She goes out into the field in search of food, but it has been totally picked over. She manages to find a root in the ground, grabs it, holds it up to the sky, and declares, "As God is my witness, they're not going to lick me. I'm going to live through this, and when it's all over I'll never be hungry again. No, nor any of my folk.... As God is my witness, I'll never be hungry again."

That's how I felt. At that moment, I made up my mind that I was going to make it on my own. I knew that if I put all of my energy into building an independent consulting practice, I would be financially independent and never have to worry about losing a job again.

More than seventeen years have passed since that day, and I have never looked back. I am not the world's most brilliant marketer, salesperson, or consultant. But I have learned over the years what it takes to make it as an independent consultant. Through a combination of continuous learning from my fellow consulting colleagues, trial and error, and perspiration, I have made myself into a successful, valuable consultant. And you can too.

It's not rocket science. All you need is the willingness to expand your comfort zone, learn, work hard, and meet the needs of clients.

You may ask, "To get started, do I need to incorporate, have a website, a separate checking account, or disability insurance?" You will most likely need to consider them all eventually, but the truth is you don't need any of these things to get started. You need only two things: a client and a method for finding more clients. This book will provide you with everything else you need to know to get started.

If you are already an independent consultant, this book will help you to accelerate your practice. It will discuss how other consultants have been able to grow their businesses into vibrant and dependable sources of continuous income.

Who will benefit from reading this book?

❏ **The Restless Employee:** Employees who are tired of working for someone else and the shackles of the corporate world, and who are willing to take a risk with their professional lives. What you hold in your hand is a guidebook for those who are sick and tired of having their work schedule and activities dictated by someone else. This book will help those who long for more control over how, where, and when they work to decide if the time is right to leave their job.

▫ **Those Seeking Financial Independence:** Wouldn't it be nice if you didn't have to worry about being laid off because the company where you work merged with or was acquired by another company, or decided to downsize, or your boss didn't like you, or your employer was being outsmarted by the competition? As an independent consultant, you call the shots. You determine your own destiny.

▫ **Those Desiring More Income:** A career in consulting can be much more lucrative than working for a corporation. Think about it. Your employer is making a profit from your work. It stands to reason that if you can satisfy the needs of customers without an employer, you can keep your share (i.e., the salary you earned as an employee), as well as your employer's share (the profit).

▫ **The Wannabe Consultant:** Although working for yourself has always been a desire of yours, it has been on the back burner. The pressures of monthly bills, mortgage, car payments, college tuition, health insurance, and saving for retirement have made the idea of working for yourself seem too impractical and unrealistic. This book will provide you with the tools you need to make the leap. It will demystify marketing and sales and show you how many others have successfully started and sustained independent consulting businesses.

▫ **The Independent Consultant at an Early Career Stage:** You still haven't quite figured out how to get to the next level of your consulting career. The allure of a monthly paycheck is tempting you to return to the corporate world, but you are not ready to give up on your dream of making your consulting business viable. You want to increase your income and make certain you are doing everything possible to stay independent.

▫ **The Experienced Consultant Seeking New Energy and Methods:** You have tasted the good life of independence and are not looking back. You know that the key to your success is to refine your consulting skills. Your goal now is to keep your business alive and growing. What you need is to learn new techniques from experienced consultants that will help you to propel your business forward.

▢ **Junior Consultants Working in Consulting Firms:** You work for a successful consulting firm. Senior consultants expect you to do most of the work. Other consultants have refined the methods you use. You realize that the only way to get ahead in your firm is to learn how to market and sell so that you can be the rainmaker.

▢ **Senior Consultants Working in Consulting Firms:** You understand that in order to continue to grow your consulting practice, you need to get back to the basics of marketing and selling. This book will provide you with insights from the perspective of the solo consultant that will help you get back to the only two things that matter in your work: selling consulting services and keeping your clients satisfied.

Each chapter is self-contained; the book does not have to be read in one sitting and can be used as a reference to address a particular problem. Each chapter focuses on a particular challenge faced by independent consultants (e.g., establishing credibility, staying focused and motivated, and setting the appropriate fees) and is organized in the following way:

▢   **Introduction:** Each chapter begins with a story that demonstrates a particular challenge faced by a real, live independent consultant.

▢   **The Challenge:** This section describes the challenge in more detail.

▢   **Solutions:** A number of different ways to overcome the challenge are then presented.

▢   **Conclusion:** This section summarizes the challenge and the solutions.

Throughout this book I will share the experiences of other consultants and the lessons they learned the hard way. In addition, we conducted a survey of two hundred independent consultants to learn how they got started and what has helped them to become successful. The results of that survey are interspersed throughout the book.

So find a comfortable chair, sit back, and enjoy reading *An Insider's Guide to Building a Successful Consulting Practice.* It could change your life. I encourage you to have a pen and a notepad nearby—not to take notes, but to start a to-do list. Include items that will accelerate your consulting business and make a personal commitment that you will follow through on each one of them until completion.

If I did it, you can too.

Introduction to The Consulting 200

In preparation for this book, a Web-based survey was sent to established independent consultants. The survey asked a variety of questions about:

□ The type of consulting practice they operate

□ How they got started

□ How they feel their consulting life compares to their former corporate life

□ How they market their services

□ What advice they would offer to new consultants

The survey was e-mailed to 368 consultants I have met over the years while networking with other independent consultants in the New England area. Two hundred responded, yielding an excellent response rate of 54 percent. Although this is by no means a statistically representative random sampling of all independent consultants, it does include consultants in many different specialty areas who have developed and established thriving businesses. Here are a few characteristics of the sample:

□ 78 percent have been an independent consultant for more than five years.

□ 7 percent started their consulting business before the age of thirty, 71 percent started between the ages of thirty and fifty, and 22 percent started after age fifty.

□ 80 percent work out of an office in their home.

□ 73 percent are solo practitioners, and 18 percent own firms that have at least one employee other than themselves.

□ 63 percent had never worked for a consulting firm before starting their own consulting business.

- The industry sectors The Consulting 200 serve most frequently include financial services, computer hardware, software, and business services (e.g., advertising, marketing, consulting, legal, printing, and staffing).

- 41 percent earn more than $100,000 per year from their consulting work, with 12 percent earning more than $200,000.

PART 1

Charging Your Battery

CHAPTER 1

Deciding Which is Best for You: Employee, Contractor, or Consultant

THE FOLLOWING THREE COLLEAGUES of mine all perform essentially the same work, but the first is an employee, the second a contractor, and the third an independent consultant. As will be the case for many of our stories, their names have been changed to protect their anonymity.

Mark is an executive search professional. He has worked for a twenty-five-person executive search firm for the past ten years. His job has two parts. First, he finds organizations that need help hiring an engineering professional. He then finds an appropriate engineer to fill the position. Mark typically works a forty-hour workweek and rarely works nights or weekends. He is paid a salary. His employer offers a pleasant working environment, all the office equipment he needs, marketing support, a 401(k) plan, and health benefits. He values the strong reputation the company has established over the past twenty years. He works side by side with other search professionals and likes the camaraderie and support he receives from them. He also likes being part of a team. He knows that his job is secure as long as he continues to do his job well, but he is also a realist. He knows that he could lose his job at any time if his sales drop, the company experiences financial difficulties, or is acquired by another firm.

Rhonda is also an executive search professional. She specializes in the high-tech industry and works as an independent contractor. Her typical assignment is a three- to six-month contract for a start-up firm or a rapidly expanding company. They usually issue her a contractor's name badge, assign her temporary office space, and agree to pay her by the hour for the time she spends recruiting for them. Rhonda enjoys her independence and likes the fact that she is removed from the politics of her clients. She is free to just do her work and leave. She typically receives more money per hour than the full-time employees, but no health or retirement benefits. The major challenge she faces is that when an assignment ends, she must then spend time marketing herself to other firms. There is often, therefore, a gap in her income.

Harvey is also an executive search professional. He has been an independent consultant for the past twenty-five years. He works out of a comfortable, well-equipped office in his home. His typical clients are owners of small, privately held businesses in need of a chief operating officer (COO). After finding a COO, Harvey works with the owners to make sure the new hire is successfully integrated into their company. Harvey relishes his independence and the control he has over his life. He spends a good deal of time volunteering for professional and community associations and traveling with his family. His wife is an employee of a large healthcare company, so his benefits are covered. He must, however, supplement their retirement savings from his own earnings. When he lands a new client, he receives significantly more money than he would if he worked in-house for a firm or as a contractor. The income he receives, though, is sporadic. During good years, cash flow is very strong, but during lean years he must draw upon his savings.

The Challenge

These three executive search professionals all apply their skills in different ways. Mark is an employee, Rhonda is a contractor, and Harvey is an independent consultant. Each type of employment has advantages and disadvantages. Before you jump full-steam ahead into consulting, you should carefully consider which of these three types is best for you. Table 1-1 compares ten major job factors you should take into consideration as you decide. Each of the factors is then described below the table.

TABLE 1-1. COMPARISON OF EMPLOYMENT, CONTRACTING, AND CONSULTING ON TEN KEY JOB FACTORS.

	EMPLOYEE	CONTRACTOR	CONSULTANT
Control of Time	Low	Low	High
Control of Space	Low	Low	High
Control of Work Activities	Low	Low	High
Stimulation from Others	High	Medium	Low
Need to Market and Sell	Low	Medium	High
Personal Growth	Varies	Medium	High
Potential for Higher Income	Low	Medium	High
Benefits	High	Low	Low
Job Security	High	Low	Low
Career Security	Low	Medium	High

Control of Time. Do you mind having set workdays and hours, or would you prefer to have more control over your time?

Most employees are restricted to set working hours and are limited to a certain number of vacation days, sick days, and personal days. Although you won't find it written in any company handbook, salaried employees are typically expected to work more than a forty-hour week and put in some time on nights and weekends as well. Some salaried employees are provided with flexibility in terms of when they start their day and when they end it, but most are not. Some have the flexibility to be able to take off in the middle of the day to run errands or attend a child's soccer game, but most do not.

Typically, contractors do not have a great deal of control over their work hours either. In Rhonda's case, she is expected, although not required, to work forty hours per week during normal working hours, making calls and interviewing job candidates. Because they use equipment that is maintained by full-time employees or because they must often attend meetings with employees of the firm, engineers hired on a contract basis are also usually restricted to working during normal work hours. I know many contract career counselors who conduct hour-long sessions with job seekers and work for an outplacement firm; their hours are restricted to standard working hours.

Some contractors, however, have more control of their time. For example, my brother-in-law was a contract programmer for Lotus for many years. He worked on an hourly basis, primarily from his home. He typically put in many more than forty hours per week, but he was able to decide exactly when he was going to work. He was free to sleep late, take off in the middle of the day, or work all night if he preferred. It was up to him.

Independent consultants can have a great deal of control over their time. They don't have bosses telling them when to arrive and how many hours they should spend working during the week. Harvey is therefore in total control of his work hours. When he is busy with client work, he puts in more hours, but he decides when. If he wants to play tennis at 3:00 PM, he is free to do so. If he wants to take a day off to visit his daughter, there is nobody saying he can't. He just needs to make sure that he is meeting the expectations he has negotiated with his clients.

But not all consultants have total control over their time. As we will discuss in chapter 4, some independent consultants adopt business models that require them to work set hours. For example, some human resource consultants work onsite during normal working hours.

Even consultants who charge by the hour can control their time, though. For example, Martin, a consultant colleague of mine, helps people use their computers. He charges by the hour for his services. A few years ago, he decided to prioritize improving his overall health over retaining any single client and decided that he wanted to reserve every morning for exercise. This meant that his earliest client appointment time became 11:00 AM. He gradually weaned his relatively few early morning clients to later hours in the day. As an independent consultant, this is something he could do because he is in total control. As it turned out, once he explained why he was making the change, he did not lose any clients.

Control of Space. Do you like the idea of having a place to go to work every day that clearly separates your work from your home? Or would you prefer to work at home or in an office that you rent for yourself?

Many independent consultants choose to leave the corporate world so they can escape the daily grind of being in an office all day, every day. They yearn for the freedom to work from home, their own office, or the local Wi-Fi–enabled coffeehouse.

Some contractors are able to work from home, but many are not. It depends on the type of work they perform and what their clients prefer. For instance, some contract programmers must work onsite because they use that organization's computer facilities or interact with employees.

Most employees do not have control over their workspace. They are required to be at the workplace during normal working hours. For many, this involves a long, expensive commute.

Depending on their work activities, some employees can telecommute (i.e., work from home periodically). This has become more common. Companies are trying to reduce the costs of office space, and they realize that most employees typically communicate with each other via e-mail rather than face-to-face. Many organizations have also realized that their fears that employees won't be productive working from home are unfounded. A survey conducted in 2007 by Citrix Online found that 23 percent of American workers regularly do their jobs from someplace besides the office. The study also found that the majority of employees envy those who work from home. Sixty-two percent of respondents who cannot work off-site said they would like to.

Control of Work Activities. Do you mind being told what to do by your boss, or would you prefer to have more control over the type of work you perform?

Some workers are attracted to consulting because they are tired of having their employers assign them work that is not challenging and does not capitalize on their skills or jibe with their current interests. Although contractors can choose whether or not to accept a contracting assignment, they are often assigned work and do not have a great deal of say in the matter.

Stimulation from Others. Do you like working as part of a work-group, team, department, and organization, or would you prefer to work alone?

This is one of the most underrated characteristics of a job. In my consulting work, I often conduct focus groups with employees to ask them about what they like and don't like about their work. They almost always say that what they like most is "the people." When I counsel people who were recently laid off from their jobs, many of them are mourning the loss of their colleagues and friends at work. They worry that those relationships will be difficult to maintain or replace.

At the same time, many employees are attracted to contracting and independent consulting in order to escape the politics and the hassles of dealing with uncooperative coworkers. One of the major challenges for many independent consultants is fighting loneliness and lack of stimulation from coworkers. There is usually no one in the office to have coffee with or speak to at the watercooler. These consultants must find other ways to meet their needs for social stimulation.

Aspiring consultants need to take stock and decide whether they will be able to feel comfortable working alone for long hours at a time, or whether they would rather be in the company of others.

Need to Market and Sell. Do you relish the idea of marketing and selling your services, or does the thought turn your stomach?

There are no two ways about it: Independent consultants and contractors need to market and sell their services. Most employees, except of course for marketing and sales professionals, do not need to do so. If you are unwilling to accept the challenge, independent consulting and contracting may not be for you.

Personal Growth. Is developing your skills and abilities important to you?

Continuously developing one's skills and abilities is very important to many employees. They become restless and frustrated when they feel they are stagnating and complain when their company does not provide them with training or professional development opportunities. Many also like to be involved in cutting-edge work.

Independent consulting does not necessarily bring these opportunities. If staying on the cutting edge in your field requires a huge investment in capital equipment, independent consulting might not be a viable option. For example, if you are a rocket scientist, you probably are going to need to be employed by a company that can afford a few rockets for you to play with.

Similarly, if you relish the type of learning that only happens through working side by side with colleagues on a daily basis, solo consulting will not meet your needs. You might want, instead, to start a consulting firm and surround yourself with industry experts.

Contracting may also limit personal growth opportunities. Although there are exceptions, many contractors complain that they are asked to do the more routine, less challenging work while full-time employees complete the more interesting tasks.

To continue to grow, independent consultants must arrange to attend professional development programs, pay for their own training, pay to attend conferences, and take the initiative to learn on their own. However, many consultants actually grow professionally because they must learn to fend for themselves. They must tend to tasks that their company did for them, such as procuring office furniture, sending out bills, keeping the books, paying payroll taxes, installing their own software, fixing the office equipment, and, of course, marketing and selling.

Potential for Higher Income. Are you satisfied with your income, or do you believe that you could earn much more if you were out on your own?

Many venture into consulting to earn more money than they could as an employee. They are tired of being stuck in jobs with restricted salary ranges, frustrated by their lack of promotions, and angered by the fact that there is no link between their pay and the quality of their job performance. They believe in themselves and are willing to take the risk of going it on their own.

One must be realistic about the potential for higher income. It may happen eventually, but it could take some time to develop the business. Although you may have some good years, your business may flounder in others.

Benefits. Are you willing to pay for your own health insurance and retirement benefits, or does the thought of having to pay for your own benefits terrify you?

For most salaried employees, benefits are a significant component of the compensation package. Employers typically spend 25 to 45 percent of an employee's salary for benefits such as health, disability, unemployment, and life insurance; retirement benefits; and many other perks that employees often take for granted (e.g., the Christmas party, free parking, and occasional free meals). As we will explore in the next chapter, this means that to maintain the salary level you earned as an employee, you must actually earn a great deal more in order to fund your own benefits.

But there are several ways for independent consultants and contractors to cope. For example, many consultants have working spouses whose organizations provide them with generous benefits that cover the entire family—including you.

Also, as an independent consultant you can purchase most of the benefits employers offer. There are many group health insurance plans you can join and insurers that will sell health insurance to individuals. It won't be inexpensive, but if you are willing to pay higher deductibles and co-payments, you can reduce the cost. And here's a real plus. If you are self-employed, the cost of health insurance may be a deductible business expense from your federal and state income taxes. This can reduce the cost greatly, depending on your tax bracket.

Job Security. Are you willing to give up the security of a full-time job?

Many wannabe consultants decide against becoming independent consultants because they don't want to lose the security that comes with a full-time job. They value monthly paychecks, paid benefits, and the certainty of long-term employment.

However, these days *job security* has become an oxymoron. Employees lose their jobs every day through no fault of their own. During difficult economic times, after a merger or acquisition, or because of a change in company strategy, even good performers are shown the door. Layoffs used to be mainly reserved for nonprofessional staff, but that is no longer the case. Companies often eliminate entire levels of management to save costs. Even the most senior managers of a firm are vulnerable.

It used to be that staying with an organization for a long time would ensure your eligibility to receive a generous pension. These days, however, very few companies still offer pensions. According to a 2007 report by McKinsey & Company, the share of active workers covered by defined benefit plans (i.e., pensions) dropped by more than half since 1980, to 20 percent.[1]

Those who are avoiding consulting due to pseudo–job security should think twice. White-collar professionals who lose their jobs are often unemployed for long periods of time while they search for their next job. The unemployment benefits they receive usually fall far short of their needs.

Career Security. Do you want security in your career?

Contrary to what you might think, many choose the life of independent consultancy for the same reason that many others remain employees—security. Consultants realize that although they don't have the security of a guaranteed paycheck, they can be confident in the fact that they won't be fired, downsized, or laid off. The worst that can happen is that they lose a client or hit a dry spell.

Career security also means that you don't have to worry about being relocated by your company to a different part of the country or, for that matter, to a different country. You also don't have to worry that if you lose your job you might have to relocate in order to take a similar job.

With the benefit of career security, independent consultants can plant roots in their community and not have to worry about a relocation that would require them to buy a new home, force their children to switch schools, and become accustomed to a new neighborhood.

Solutions

So, what's it going to be: employee, contractor, or consultant? Which is right for you? Here are eight steps you can take to help you decide.

---

1 *The Coming Shakeout in the Defined Benefit Market*, Research Report produced by McKinsey & Company, 2007, p. 6.

Survey Results: Why Be Independent?

Here's what The Consulting 200 said when asked why they first started as independent consultants. As you can see, control was the key issue. They wanted more control over the type of work they performed and their time.

I first started as an independent consultant because:

Percent *(Multiple answers allowed)*

62	I wanted more control over the type of work I performed.
60	I wanted more control over my time.
53	I wanted greater personal growth.
53	I didn't want to have to work for anyone.
45	I relished the challenge of self-employment.
41	I wanted the potential of earning more money.
26	I was laid off or fired.
23	I wanted more control over my workspace.
14	I didn't want to have to worry about finding a job.
12	I wanted to work only part-time.
9	I didn't want to worry about relocating.

Hire a Career Counselor

Everyone needs to step back periodically and take an objective look at his or her career. A career counselor can help you more clearly understand what's important to you. If you are thinking about making a major change, such as changing jobs, changing careers, or striking out on your own, a career counselor can help you think it all through. To find a good counselor, ask your colleagues for a personal recommendation. You might also contact the National Career Development Association (www.ncda.org) or the National Board of Certified Counselors (www.nbcc.org) for lists of reputable counselors. Then meet with the counselor to see if there is a good fit.

Talk to Independent Consultants

You probably know many independent consultants, either through work or socially. Most consultants are happy to talk about their work and their career choice. Offer to buy lunch and then pepper the consultant with questions like, "Why did you decide to become an independent consultant?" "What challenges did you face at the start?" "What do you like most about consulting?" "What do you like least?" Also, ask about the ten factors described in Table 1-1. For example, "Do you feel like you have control of your time, your space, and your activities?" "How do you feel about having to market and sell?" "What do you do about combating loneliness?"

Talk to Colleagues Who May Have Considered or Dabbled in Consulting

You probably also know several coworkers who are former independent consultants or who seriously considered consulting. I wouldn't ask your boss (unless you have a very close friendship with him or her outside of work), but others would probably be glad to answer your questions.

Talk to Contractors

There is a good chance that your company hires contractors in your field. Ask them what they like and don't like about contracting. Ask them why they are a contractor rather than an independent consultant.

Examine Your Tolerance for Risk

Some people have a very difficult time taking risks in their personal or professional lives. Seriously consider whether you are too risk adverse to make a major career change. Then again, even if you are risk averse, this may be a good time for you to get over your fears. Lining up a client or two ahead of time may provide you with the confidence you need to take the plunge.

Ease into Consulting

Many independent consultants started their practices by moonlighting while they were fully employed. They started consulting at night, on weekends, and during vacations. Once they had a solid cadre of business, they were able to leave their jobs and consult full time.

Consider Working for a Consulting Firm First

You may need to take baby steps before you take the leap into consulting. Consider working for a consulting firm to gain the experience you need before eventually venturing out on your own. It is important, though, that you make certain you do more in the firm

Survey Results: Comparison of Independent Consulting to Last Job on Several Key Job Factors

The Consulting 200 was asked to compare their lives as independent consultants to their last full-time jobs. They report they have more control over their time and space and are happier. They do, however, have less generous benefits and less stimulation from others.

Percent Agreement*	Compared to my last full-time job, as an independent consultant, now:
91	I have more control over my space (i.e., where I work).
90	I am happier.
88	I have more control over my work activities (i.e., the type of projects or work I conduct).
86	I have more control over my time (i.e., when I work).
72	I have a greater potential for higher income.
70	I have better career security (i.e., not having to worry about relocating or changing my profession).
69	I have more opportunity to develop my skills and abilities.
54	I have better job security (i.e., not having to worry about losing a job or going out of business).
40	I have more stimulation from others (i.e., social stimulation from working and/or interacting with others).
10	I have better employee benefits (i.e., health and retirement benefits).

*The percentage who strongly agreed or agreed with the statement using a 5-point response scale of Strongly Agree, Agree, Partly Agree/Partly Disagree, Disagree, and Strongly Disagree.

than just execute projects that other people sell. You need to learn how to write proposals, market and sell, and manage clients. For those reasons, it may be better for you to work for a small firm rather than a large one. Be careful about signing noncompete agreements that limit your ability to eventually leave the firm and start your own.

Continue Reading This Book

This book will provide you with the insights you need to become an independent consultant. We are starting off slowly. This first chapter discussed whether consulting is right for you. In the next chapter, we will talk more about something that is probably foremost in your mind: the economic realities of independent consulting.

Conclusion

Take a realistic look at what is most important to you (e.g., control of your time and space, the potential for a higher income, and job security) and then decide whether employment, contracting, or independent consulting will enable you to achieve what you most value.

If you want a steady paycheck, job security, and ongoing social contact with peers, then perhaps it is best for you to remain an employee.

If you want some control of your time and space and the security of a long-term contract, and you are willing to market and sell yourself, then perhaps contracting is right for you.

But if you want complete freedom and an unlimited potential for income, then independent consulting may be the answer.

CHAPTER 2

Understanding the Economic Realities of Independent Consulting

S TILL WITH ME? Is independent consulting still a real possibility for you? If so, let's consider the sobering economic realities.

Ellen, a documentary film producer, worked for many years as a contractor for a public relations firm in Chicago. She created many wonderful short films for the firm's pharmaceutical and nonprofit clients. She loved the work and appreciated the fact that she didn't have to do any of the marketing or selling herself. Unfortunately, she was paid by the hour at a fairly low rate. She was able to work a lot of days, but it required an uncompensated two-hour commute each way to the downtown office. Also, she hadn't received a substantial raise in many years.

She yearned to be independent, work out of her home, and earn more money. Over the years she did land several clients on her own while she was still also contracting with the PR firm. Unfortunately, she suffered from what my sales consultant colleagues call, "head trash." She quoted fees that were very low. She did this because she desperately wanted the business, devalued her own skills, wasn't aware of what other people were charging, and lacked enough "chutzpah" to charge a healthy fee. She felt if she charged more, she wouldn't win the business. As a result, expenses for camera crews, editing studio time, and travel left her with very little profit.

The Challenge

You've got to be able to charge enough for your services to make it worth your while. If you don't, your consulting practice will never succeed. Consultants often don't charge enough because they:

- Don't understand the value their work has for their clients
- Have little understanding of what other consultants charge
- Are scared of not having any business
- Lack plain old chutzpah

If you can't charge enough to make it worth your while:

- Your clients may not need your services.
- You may need to reduce your own expenses.
- Consulting may not be the right career choice for you.

Survey Results: Level of Income

As shown below, approximately three-fourths of The Consulting 200 were able to support themselves primarily from their consulting work in their first years as independent consultants.

During my first year as an independent consultant, I was able to support myself primarily:

Percent *(Multiple answers allowed)*

74	From my consulting work
29	From the income of my spouse or significant other
20	From my personal savings
12	From the severance I received from my former company
3	By taking out a business loan from a bank or other financial institution
2	By borrowing money from friends or relatives
1	By taking out an equity loan on my home

You also might be seriously underestimating how much you need to charge in order to achieve your income goals. Consider the following example. Let's say, for the sake of round numbers, that you want or need an income of approximately $100,000 before personal income taxes. As shown in Table 2-1, as an independent consultant you are going to have to receive much more than $100,000 from your clients in order to achieve that level of income. The numbers, based on my conversations with my accountant, Curtis Feldman, a CPA and a partner in the firm, Shepherd and Goldstein (www.sgllp.com), are approximate and not all-inclusive, but they make the point effectively.

TABLE 2-1. APPROXIMATE DOLLARS NEEDED TO ACHIEVE A CONSULTING INCOME OF $100,000.

$100,000	**Desired net income goal (before income taxes)**
15,000	Self-employment taxes (Social Security and Medicare)
15,000	Health benefits (for you and your family)
15,000	Retirement benefits
7,500	Other benefits (e.g., disability insurance and life insurance)
10,000	Office expenses (e.g., equipment, postage, and supplies)
2,500	Automobile expenses
7,500	Marketing expenses
2,500	Educational expenses
$175,000	**Total revenue needed to achieve desired net income goal**

Self-Employment Taxes. At the time of this writing (2009), as an employee you pay 6.2 percent in Social Security taxes and your employer matches that with 6.2 percent on the first $106,800 of income. In addition, you pay 1.45 percent for Medicare, and your employer, again, matches with 1.45 percent on all earnings. As an independent consultant, however, you will have to pay not only *all* the Social Security, but the Medicare payments as well—for a total of 15.3 percent.

Health Benefits. Contrary to popular belief, you don't have to be employed to have healthcare insurance. Of course, it is not inexpensive, but you can purchase healthcare benefits from many insurance companies. The premiums will depend on such factors as whether you enroll as part of a group or as an individual, whether you are single or part of a family, the type of coverage you select, and the deductible and co-payment amounts. There are many organizations you can join that will enable you to purchase good plans at group rates. To avoid sticker shock when you are shopping for health insurance, remember that it probably wasn't totally free at your last job. Many employees pay 50 percent or more of the premiums each month.

Retirement Benefits. Don't overlook this expense. Just because you are self-employed doesn't mean you don't need to save for retirement. Your last company may have contributed to or matched the contributions you made to your 401(k) or other defined contribution program. You will now have to pay it all. If you were fortunate enough to work for a company that had a pension (i.e., a defined benefit program), you will need to create your own. There are many financial advisers who can help you establish these programs. Your contributions to your retirement are deductible from your income taxes. A further advantage of self-employment is that you can create a plan that will enable you to save more before-tax income than you probably would be able to do as an employee. For example, if you establish a profit-sharing plan, you can save 15 to 25 percent of your profit. You can also set up your own defined benefit retirement program and, depending on your age and other factors, save quite a bit more of your before-tax income.

Other Benefits. There are a host of other benefits that may be important to you as well. You will need to decide whether it is important to purchase dental insurance, eye care insurance, disability insurance, errors of omission insurance, liability insurance, life insurance, etc. When your employer paid for these, it was a no-brainer. Now that you have to pay for them yourself, you might want to give careful thought to whether the premiums are worth the expense or whether you are willing to self-insure. You may also decide to wait until your business picks up steam before you take on these additional expenses.

Survey Results: Funding Retirement

As shown below, about half of The Consulting 200 contributed to their retirement plan during the first year of their business and half did not.

During the first year of my consulting business:

Percent *(Multiple answers allowed)*

31	I didn't have a retirement plan.
30	I had a plan and contributed partially.
22	I had a plan and contributed fully.
17	I had a plan but did not contribute.

Office Expenses. You need to plan for your business expenses. Every consulting practice differs in terms of what expenses it will incur, but many expenses are common to all service businesses. For instance, you will now have to pay for the pens, pencils, and paper clips that used to somehow appear in your home from your employer. You will also need to pay for postage, telephone, Internet access, computer equipment, and computer supplies.

Automobile Expenses. Although you won't be commuting to work, you will be using your car to visit clients and prospects, meet with colleagues, and attend professional meetings. These expenses, which include the cost of gasoline, maintenance, and repairs, can be high. Your business use of your automobile, though, is a deductible business expense.

Marketing Expenses. You will also need to pay for marketing expenses such as Web design, printing, stationery, postage, and networking (i.e., entertaining clients and prospects).

Educational Expenses. It is important that you budget for membership in professional organizations, attendance at professional meetings, subscriptions to professional journals, and other educational expenses, such as books, DVDs, CDs, videos, Podcasts, and Webinars.

Survey Results: Insurance Coverage

The majority of The Consulting 200 did not immediately run out and purchase every possible type of insurance coverage when they launched their businesses. Some were covered for health and dental care under their spouse's plan, and some went without. A third or less purchased disability, errors and omissions, or liability insurance. Approximately one-third purchased none of these types of insurance at all.

During the first year of my consulting business, I purchased:

Percent *(Multiple answers allowed)*

52	Medical insurance
30	Disability insurance
27	Liability insurance
14	Errors and omission insurance
13	Dental insurance
31	None of the above

As if this isn't enough to make you lose sleep at night, after paying all of these expenses you will still need to pay individual income taxes out of the $100,000 you have managed to keep for yourself.

Solutions

Here are a few critical steps you should take before blindly assuming that as an independent consultant you will earn enough money to support the business and your family.

Do the Math

You need to be pragmatic about whether your plan for your consulting business is realistic. Let's say, for example, that a consultant plans to start an executive coaching practice. She plans to counsel clients in her office and charge them by the hour. (We'll discuss in chapter 4 why charging by the hour is probably not a good idea.) Table 2-2 provides a realistic estimate of how many consulting days she will be able to charge clients.

TABLE 2-2. CALCULATION OF APPROXIMATE NUMBER OF AVAILABLE CONSULTING DAYS.

Number of working days in a year (52 weeks x 5 days)	260
Approximate number of holidays	-14
Approximate number of vacation days	-20
Approximate number of sick and personal days	-5
Two days per 48 weeks for marketing, sales, and administrative work	-96
Remaining days available for you to bill clients	**125**

Say she decides to charge $100 per hour. That's $800 per day. Assuming she can find enough clients to pay for all of her available eight hours for 125 days, that comes to $100,000.

This may be fine for her, but it is well short of the goal of $175,000 we discussed above. In order for her to achieve that goal, she would need to charge $1,400 per day, or $175 per hour. If she doesn't think people will pay that much, or if she doesn't think that she will be able to fill up her calendar with clients, then she is going to have to rethink her business plan.

Consider another example. Let's say that a public relations consultant plans to offer his services on a retainer basis. He plans to charge $2,500 per month (or $30,000 per year) to clients. In order to reach his goal of $175,000, he is going to have to do business with six clients throughout the year. He must decide whether that is a realistic goal. If not, he needs to charge more, develop a different service, or abandon the plan.

Make Certain You Charge Enough

Even after doing the math and knowing what they need to charge in order to achieve the income they desire, many beginning consultants charge too little. They do so because they have the following mistaken beliefs:

It is better to have a low-paying client than no client at all. Nothing could be further from the truth. If you want your business to work, you have to be able to charge clients enough money to make it worth your while. The numbers have to add up. This is not a time to gain experience. If you don't have enough experience to meet clients' needs, then you should get that experience as an employee.

A low fee will help you win business over clients who charge more. Trying to make a living as a consultant by being the low bidder is a prescription for disaster. You've got to believe that you are going to help your clients and that your work is worth the money you charge. You are not in a commodity business. Hopefully you are providing high-quality services to your clients. If anything, you want to be perceived as the high-cost provider rather than the low-cost provider. It is vitally important for you to adopt this mindset.

Since you are just starting out, you can't charge that much. How long you have been consulting should have little impact on how much you charge. What is more important is how well you solve the problems of your clients. I have a colleague who left a large executive compensation consulting firm to start his own business. When he was with the large firm, he charged $4,000 per day. When he started on his own, even though he provided the same services to clients and achieved the same results, he believed that he should charge less because his overhead was lower and he didn't have his former firm's reputation behind him. Why shouldn't he have continued to charge $4,000 per day or more? He was selling himself short.

If you start off with a low fee and do good work, you will be able to raise your rates. This is a common misconception. Let's say that to land the account, you charge a client $20,000 for a project, knowing that is about half what other firms charge for similar work. The client is pleased with your work, and the next year they approach you about conducting the same project again. It is unlikely that you will be able to double your fee. The client already believes that the work is worth only $20,000. Why? Because that's what you initially told them it was worth.

Conduct Market Intelligence

Your fees should be based on both what your services are worth to your clients and what you need to make your business succeed. What others charge for similar services is secondary, although it is certainly important information to have. Wouldn't it be useful to know that your competitors are charging twice as much or half as much as you are? Undoubtedly, your prospects are going to test the market and learn what others charge, so you should too. Knowing whether you are charging below, at, or above the rates of other firms can be extremely helpful when making a bid or submitting a proposal.

Gathering this information is not easy, but not at all impossible. Consulting firms and independent firms rarely publish their fees. Even if you are bold enough to ask your competitors what they charge, they probably won't tell you.

Some consultants have success asking their losses (i.e., firms who did not select them but instead selected another firm), but I have found that such prospects don't feel comfortable sharing this information with me. Instead, I prefer to take the high road and just thank them for their time and wish them success with the firm they hired.

Others pose as shoppers or have friends or colleagues do it for them. They contact competitors and pretend they are looking for a consultant to help them with a particular project. They then ask what they charge. I know this type of behavior occurs frequently, but I personally feel it is unethical.

Here are a few other suggestions you might try.

Ask a satisfied client. Once you have established a solid relationship with a client and feel it would not jeopardize your relationship in any way, ask something like this: "Joe, I know that when we first started working together, you also talked to other consultants. It would be very helpful to my business if you could share with me what other firms charge. Is this something you would feel comfortable sharing? If not, I perfectly understand."

Ask colleagues who hire consultants. You may know people professionally or socially who hire consultants in your field. Ask them what they typically pay.

Look for Other Economic Strategies to Get You Started

It is possible, although probably unlikely, that you will achieve your income goal in your first year. You will need to fund yourself until your business kicks into full gear. Here are some potential strategies:

Survey Results: Recovery of Full Income

Less than one-quarter of The Consulting 200 were able to match their level of income at their former job during their first year of consulting. For the majority, it took two or more years.

Approximately how many years did it take you to earn the level of income you had been earning at your former job?

Percent	
43	Within two to three years
23	Within the first year
19	More than three years
15	I have not yet matched the income I received at my former job.

Borrow money. This is a dangerous strategy, which I don't recommend. Borrowing money from a family member or friend is not good for your relationship. What do you do if your business doesn't take off? You could develop a detailed business plan and submit it to a bank, but banks are very leery about providing funds for startup service businesses. They will also charge you a high interest rate.

Invest in yourself. If you honestly believe that your business can and will succeed, then instead of trying to convince others to fund your business, you should be willing to invest in yourself. Dig into your savings—though not your retirement savings—or take out an equity loan on your home. Try to avoid credit card debt, of course, as these rates are typically exorbitant.

Use your severance. When I was laid off from my job, I received a six-month severance package. This served as my seed money while I launched my consulting business. Unfortunately, many companies today aren't as generous with severance packages as they were in the past. But if you are receiving severance payments, make it last as long as you can while you are building your business.

Lean on your spouse. If you are fortunate to have a working spouse, plan on living on his or her income until your consulting income begins to flow. If your spouse is not working, now is probably a good time for him or her to look for a job.

Tighten your belt. Postpone that vacation you were planning or the purchase of a new car. Look for ways to cut your personal spending. Write out a detailed budget ahead of time so that you don't have to spend valuable time and energy worrying about money every day while you are trying to launch your business.

Hire a Good Accountant

As noted, there are many expenses you will incur as a consultant that you did not have to pay as an employee. However, there are also many deductions to your taxes that you can take as well. Here are just a few:

- The costs associated with using a portion of your home as an office (including the percentage of household expenses used in your home office for things like electricity, trash pickup, cleaning service, and security alarm services)
- All business-related expenses, including supplies, postage, telephone, and Internet access
- Depreciation of business equipment, such as desks, chairs, filing cabinets, telephones, answering machines, computers, printers, photocopiers, and fax machines
- Deductions for the business use of your car
- Marketing expenses, such as printing of stationery, business cards, brochures, and marketing materials
- Professional development expenses, such as dues for professional associations; registration fees for professional meetings; attendance at training programs; the cost of books, CDs, DVDs, and training materials related to your business; and subscriptions to professional journals
- Professional fees for your Webmaster, designer, marketing consultant, accountant, and lawyer
- A portion of the expenses associated with entertaining prospects and clients

A good accountant will make certain that you reduce your taxes by appropriately taking advantage of the opportunity to make all of these deductions.

Alter Your Strategy

You need to be practical and realistic. You may be dying to be an independent consultant. But if you've done the math and you see that it is just not practical for you to be able to charge what you need to make a go of it, then you need to reevaluate your plan. Two major strategies can have a dramatic impact on the economic viability of your consulting practice: focusing your work on a specific problem or niche, and changing your planned business model. Both are discussed in the next two chapters.

Conclusion

To succeed, you cannot view independent consulting as a hobby. You need to be a smart businessperson and carefully examine the economics of your plans with open eyes. Look at your income goals and all the expenses you will incur. Then do the math. If you see that even after a few years, your plan is unlikely to work, then proceeding anyway does not make much sense. You need to be a smart businessperson and alter your strategy instead.

CHAPTER 3

Focusing Your Work on a Specific Problem or Niche

DURING THE PAST FIFTEEN YEARS, Mark Campbell (www.mjcampbellassoc.com), a good friend and colleague, has learned the hard way how important it is for consultants to focus their work on a specific problem or niche.

For many years Mark had been a human resource professional in several major manufacturing organizations. His specialty was organizational development and training. He had many years of experience developing and delivering training programs on leadership, presentation skills, and a host of other topics. Thirsty for a new challenge, he decided to leave his job to start a training consulting business.

After struggling for several years, he discovered that training had become a commodity. He had invested a great deal of time in developing a variety of training programs in case he received a request from a client for a particular type of training. He would then customize the workshops to fit the needs of the client. But he found that he was competing with videos, CDs, and other off-the-shelf programs that his prospects could purchase for a few hundred dollars rather than the few thousand he was seeking. He also found that he was losing business to competitors who focused on one type of training rather than many. For example, he found it difficult to compete with presentation skills or time management trainers who had written books about their expertise and who had years of experience on that one topic.

Frustrated by his lack of business, he decided to go in a completely different direction. Many of his clients had been asking him to coach some of their senior executives. Coaching was a skill that Mark had acquired as a human resource professional. He enjoyed it and knew that he was good at it. He therefore decided to rebrand himself as an executive coach and focus on providing executive coaching services.

During the first year of marketing his coaching services, he was again challenged by the fact that he was competing with many types of professionals for the same work: former athletic coaches, psychologists, and the many people who had earned certifications from the various new credentialing groups that had emerged.

What he needed was a hook, something that would make him unique and special. One day the answer dawned on him. For several years he had been teaching courses in the master's in healthcare management program at Harvard University. One night a week, he taught healthcare executives interested in moving into leadership roles in health care and health science organizations. Some of them had become his coaching clients. He realized that if he focused on coaching healthcare and health science executives, he would have a leg up on the many others who offered coaching to any and all types of executives.

It has been several years since Mark learned this valuable lesson. His business is thriving. He has worked for some of the most prestigious firms in the industry. He has written several books on the topic and is now the go-to guy for healthcare executive coaching. "Once I *niched*," he explains, "I knew which professional meetings to attend, which journals to write articles for, who to contact for appointments, and who to send mailings to. When organizations hire an executive coach, they have a lot of fear about hiring the right consultant. By specializing in their industry, I have taken away a lot of their fear. They are able to say, 'He is one of us!'"

The moral of the story: focus, focus, focus. The more you focus, the more opportunities you will uncover.

The Challenge

Both beginning and experienced consultants often flounder because they lack a clear focus. They are unclear in their own minds about exactly what service they provide, for whom they provide it, and what results they help their clients achieve.

Some might argue that consultants should provide a wide variety of services to many different types of clients. I disagree. Here are some reasons why I believe that a clear focus is critically important:

You will lose business to those who specialize. Consultants who claim to be generalists by offering a variety of services to many different types of individuals and organizations run the risk of being viewed as jacks-of-all-trades but masters of none. For instance, who would you rather hire if your washing machine were to break down, a general contractor who claims he can fix anything or a washing machine repair specialist?

Survey Results: Generalist or Specialist: That is the Question.

Very few of The Consulting 200 consider themselves generalists. They describe themselves as either specialists or part generalists/part specialists.

Some consultants are primarily generalists, while others focus on a specific problem, industry sector, geography, or other niche. How would you describe your work?

Percent	
45	Primarily a specialist
39	Partly a generalist/partly a specialist
17	A generalist

Prospects won't remember what you do. For consultants, there are only three types of people in the world: your clients, prospects, and everyone else. "Everyone else" are the people who can lead you to new clients. With a clear focus, you will be able to articulate to them what you do. This will help them spread your message so that your name or the name of your firm will be unambiguously associated with your specialty and the results you achieve. For example, which of the following two statements provides a clearer picture of the services a consultant provides? "I provide marketing consulting services for all types of businesses." "I provide marketing services to help dental practices in Northern New Jersey who are trying to increase the number of patients they serve."

It will be difficult for you to market your services. If you know exactly the type of service you provide and realize for whom it has value, you will be able to speak and write with a clear message. You will also be able to target your message to the appropriate audience. For instance, the dental marketing consultant could purchase a list of dentists in Northern New Jersey and conduct mailings to that group, conduct speeches at the local dental association, and mingle with dentists at the monthly meetings of the local dental association. Consultants who provide marketing for all types of businesses may not know where to start their marketing activities.

You will dilute your ability to provide results. It would be a disservice to your clients if you extend your service offerings beyond what you are actually capable of successfully providing. For example, the marketing generalist could help dentists in Northern New Jersey, but there would be a steep learning curve to become knowledgeable about dentistry and to understand the marketplace. Why should the client have to pay to educate the consultant?

You won't be able to command higher fees. Specialists can command higher fees because their knowledge, expertise, and experience are highly valued. Generalists are a dime a dozen. To command higher fees, you must specialize in a particular service, problem, issue, or market. Mark Campbell could offer executive coaching services to all types of managers, but by specializing in health care, he has learned which management practices are most effective for those types of organizations. He is thus able to provide better advice.

You will have to constantly reinvent the wheel. If you focus on delivering a specific service over and over again, you will be able to use similar proposals, methods, and reports. For instance, Harvey Lemovitz (HLemovitz@fmcpartners.com) provides financial consulting services to small businesses. He serves as the CFO to these companies. His narrow specialty is working with wholesale frozen fish distributors in Eastern Massachusetts. He helps them borrow money when they make large purchases and keeps their accounts in order. His strategic advantage in the marketplace comes from the many time-tested methods and procedures he has developed to combat most of the problems and challenges his frozen fish distributor clients face.

You might think that this is a very narrow focus. But it's a great niche for him. These companies need his services, and they are too small to afford a full-time CFO. They want someone who knows their business. He has more than a dozen clients in this niche and has expanded to the point where he has brought in several partners.

You won't be able to hire employees. If you focus on a specific service, you may eventually be able to teach others how to deliver your specialized service. This will provide you with the ability to make money from the work of others. (See the *Consulting Firm* model described in chapter 4.)

It will be more difficult to maintain your passion. Maintaining motivation and energy can be very difficult for independent consultants, especially if you try to be all things to all people. You will end up taking on work that is not always to your liking. Focusing on an issue or service that is important to you will help you stay motivated.

Solutions

There are four basic ways to focus your service. You can key on a particular type of service, a specific industry sector, a geographical area, or a combination.

Focus on a Particular Service

Become the leading expert for a particular type of consulting service. For example, my colleague Ken Lizotte (www.thoughtleading.com) helps consultants get published. He helps them target business publications and book publishers who need articles and books in their subject area. He then helps them write the articles and books.

Focus on a Particular Industry Sector

Become a niche player by focusing your services on one specific industry. Develop proprietary approaches that address the unique needs of that sector. Then read what they read, attend their professional meetings, publish and advertise in their trade journals, and exhibit at their conferences.

For instance, Jeffrey Scott (www.jeffreyscott.biz) is a marketing consultant who specializes in working with small companies that provide landscaping and swimming pool installation. He grew up in this type of family business and has a great deal of experience marketing it. He found that there was a need for his expertise in other similar companies. He now writes books on the topic, speaks at landscapers' conventions, and provides coaching to owners of these businesses.

Focus on a Particular Geography

Perhaps you can develop services that uniquely fit a particular geography. Mark Campbell found that his focus on coaching healthcare and health science executives was a great fit for the Boston area, since it is one of the hotbeds for health care and health sciences. Some of the biggest and best organizations are located there.

Focus on Some Combination of the Above

For example, you could specialize in providing a particular service to a specific industry sector in a specific location. The key is to focus where there is a real need for your expertise and services.

Conclusion

Although it is tempting to try to offer as many types of services as you possibly can, I believe that it is critically important for independent consultants to focus. Sit down today and refine your business by asking yourself the following questions:

- Am I trying to do too many things for too many types of people?
- Am I crystal clear about my focus?
- Are others clear about my focus?
- How can I narrow my focus?
- How can I narrow my focus even further?

CHAPTER 4

Choosing a Business Model

F RANK IS A SENIOR HUMAN RESOURCE professional with a
wealth of experience. During his twenty-year career he held nine different HR positions at organizations ranging from large international public companies to small startups. When the work became routine, he often grew bored and looked for new challenges. He finally
decided to become an HR consultant.

His first client was a small division of a much larger international manufacturing company. He negotiated a deal so that he would
spend about thirty hours per week onsite consulting to the president
and running the HR function. While there, he helped the company
hire a junior HR person, to whom he off-loaded the day-to-day work.
That allowed him to focus on the more strategic HR activities.

He then landed another client, a small startup. This assignment
occupied the remainder of his week. Frank enjoyed working with his
two clients but gradually realized that he was not experiencing the
freedom he desired. He was not in control of his time, his space, or

his work activities. Also, since his time was fully occupied, he had no time left to market his services. Thus, he had no way to grow his consultancy or his income.

The Challenge

This is a common story. Many professionals are attracted to consulting by the allure of more freedom and higher income potential. The problem people like Frank have is that they have chosen a business model that limits their freedom and income.

A business model is a framework for operating a business, a general strategy regarding how you are going to provide value to clients, charge for your services, leverage your time, and make a certain level of income.

Consider the stories of two different consultants who discovered that the business model they were using was limiting their growth. They successfully changed the model to their benefit.

Karen left a large international human resource consulting firm to start her own business. Much like Frank, one of her first decisions was to offer her services as the in-house human resource generalist for several small clients. Also like Frank, she quickly realized that this strategy wasn't giving her the freedom or the potential for growth she desired. Her time was fully occupied, and she had no time left for marketing and sales.

She decided to change her business model. She found several other human resource professionals who were seeking part-time work as consultants. She gradually transitioned her current clients to use the services of her colleagues, while she maintained supervisory responsibility and regular contact with the clients. Most importantly, she maintained billing responsibilities, thereby gaining leverage by marking up the work of her colleagues. This afforded her more time to market and sell, and the business began to grow exponentially as Karen placed junior colleagues in the offices of all of her new clients. Soon she opened up an office outside of her home and hired several administrative assistants to help coordinate the work of all of the consultants in the field and with marketing. A real ongoing business had been born.

Mary Jones realized early on that her business model wasn't working. She is an employee benefits consultant specializing in helping companies reduce the cost of the health insurance benefits they offer to their employees. During a typical two- or three-month project, she helped her clients understand what they wanted to offer to employees, gathered bids from several insurance companies, helped her clients decide which insurance plan to use, and then helped the clients to implement the new plan.

Mary quickly realized that her business was either feast or famine. Some months she was very busy, working with several clients. This left her with little time to market her business. Consequently, when the projects ended, she had no business and had to start furiously marketing to drum up more clients.

Mary also felt that the way she could help her clients the most was by developing a long-term relationship with them rather than just conducting a short-term project. If she were able to develop this type of relationship with her clients, she would be able to gain a better understanding of the organization and how to best help them.

She therefore decided that she would no longer take on new project work. Instead, she would only work with clients on a long-term retainer basis, for a minimum of one year. The work she would perform for them would be essentially the same, but in order to maximize her value to them, fund an office, bring on junior consultants, and fund her marketing activities, she needed a long-term commitment with at least twelve months of ongoing fees.

This meant that Mary had to turn down project work in order to make her new business model work. That's what she did, and her business began to boom. With a continuous flow of income, she was able to rent an office, hire several junior consultants, and focus more time and money marketing her business.

One of the most important and often overlooked tasks for both new and experienced independent consultants is to understand their business model. This chapter describes twenty-two different consulting business models. Table 4-1 compares the models using seven criteria. Each of the criteria is then described below the table, followed by a description of each model.

Survey Results: Should I Develop a Detailed Business Plan?

Most career counselors will tell you that if you are going to start a business, you should have a detailed business plan. Sounds like wise advice, especially if you are going to try to borrow money from a financial institution to launch your business. However, as shown below, only about one-third of The Consulting 200 had such a plan.

When I started my consulting business, I developed a detailed business plan.

Percent	
67	No
33	Yes

1. Operating leverage. Just as a lever enables someone to lift a large object with little effort, a consulting practice with operating leverage enables consultants to maximize the returns on their time and effort. As a consultant, you can achieve leverage by:

1. Profiting from the work of others by hiring employees or subcontractors

2. Profiting by selling products with high markups, like materials you create yourself

3. Reusing methods or information so that you don't have to continually reinvent the wheel

Some business models afford a great deal of leverage and others provide very little.

2. Management of others required. Some consultants enter the field as experienced managers and relish the opportunity to manage employees or subcontractors. Others become consultants so that they never have to manage people again. Some of the business models require managing others and some do not.

TABLE 4-1. CONSULTING BUSINESS MODELS EVALUATED ON SEVEN CRITERIA

Consulting Business Model	Operating Leverage	Management of Others Required	Startup Time Horizon	Ongoing Marketing Required	Passive Income	Income Potential	Work/Life Balance
1. Time-Based	Low	No	Short	Low	No	Low	Low
2. Project-Based	Low	No	Short	High	No	Medium	Medium
3. Retainer-Based	Low	No	Short	Low	Yes	High	High
4. Results-Based	High	No	Short	High	No	High	High
5. Annuity	High	No	Short	Low	No	High	Medium
6. Consulting Firm	High	Yes	Medium	High	Yes	High	Medium
7. Outsourcer	High	No	Medium	Low	No	Medium	Low
8. Product Sales	High	No	Long	High	Yes	Medium	High
9. Razor Blade	High	No	Long	Medium	Yes	High	High
10. Subscription	High	No	Long	Medium	Yes	Medium	High
11. Distributor	Medium	No	Short	Medium	Yes	Low	High
12. Publisher	High	No	Long	High	Yes	High	High
13. Franchiser	High	Yes	Long	High	Yes	High	High
14. Franchisee	Low	No	Short	High	No	Low	Medium
15. Strategic Relationship	Low	No	Short	Medium	No	Low	Low
16. General Contractor	High	Yes	Medium	High	Yes	High	Medium
17. Subcontractor	Low	No	Short	Low	No	Low	Low
18. Freemium	High	No	Long	High	Yes	High	Medium
19. Association	High	Yes	Long	Medium	Yes	Medium	High
20. Speaking	Low	No	Short	High	No	Low	Low
21. Public Seminar	Low	Yes	Long	High	No	Low	Low
22. Author	High	No	Long	High	Yes	Low	High

3. Startup time horizon. A number of the business models can be started immediately, while others require the investment of time for up-front development of products or services.

4. Ongoing marketing required. Some consultants disdain marketing their services, and others relish it. Needless to say, if you don't do any marketing, you will soon be an ex-consultant. However, some business models require less ongoing marketing than others.

5. Passive income. Wouldn't it be nice to sit back in your favorite armchair and just count your money as it flows to you? This is the idea underlying several of the business models.

6. Income potential. Many independent consultants are happy with just enough income to pay their current bills or to match the salary from their last job. Others want to earn considerably more. Some of the consulting models have the potential for producing a high level of income, while others do not.

Survey Results: How Do Consultants Charge for Their Services?

Consultants don't stick to one method of charging clients. The majority charge both for their time and by the project, depending on the client and the type of service they are delivering. Far fewer charge on a retainer basis, for products or subscriptions, or for the economic value of the results they achieve.

I receive consulting income by charging:

Percent	(Multiple answers allowed)
80	By the project
67	For my time (i.e., by the hour or day)
39	On a retainer basis
15	For products or subscriptions
13	Based on the economic value of the results I achieve for my clients
7	In other ways

7. Work/life balance. Many choose independent consulting because they want to achieve a better balance between work and the rest of their life. They are seeking control of their time (when they work) and their space (where they work). Some of the business models afford a greater opportunity to achieve this balance.

Each of the twenty-two business models is described below. Each has it advantages and disadvantages.

1. Time-Based Model. One of the most common and simplest consulting business models involves charging for time. At the beginning of the engagement, an hourly or daily rate, as well as the scope of the work, is set with the client. The rate is based on such factors as what others are typically charging for a similar service ("the going rate"), but also the income the consultant needs to meet his or her income needs and to sustain the business itself.

Martin Kadansky (www.kadansky.com) helps people use their computers. He teaches his clients how to better use their software and how to deal with computer problems as they arise. He charges by the hour. He prefers this approach because he never knows how long any particular job is going to take, and because if he helps one client learn about e-mail attachments and another how to add page numbers to a document, he likes the fairness and simplicity of charging them for his time.

The advantage of this approach is that the consultant is paid for each hour of actual work. Many consultants begin an engagement without being able to accurately predict how many hours it will take to solve the client's problem. With this approach, they need not be concerned about not being compensated fairly if a job takes longer than they had predicted.

Sean Majors helps manufacturers in the United States outsource production to China. He came to a "How to Charge for Your Consulting Services" session I was conducting. "I'm driving myself crazy," he told me. "I have several clients who pay me by the hour, and so I work all of the time. I'm constantly looking at the clock and counting the money as I work. I like to cut my lawn, but I can't because if I do I'll lose an hour or two of billable time. I like the money, but I want my life back!" I encouraged Sean to bill his clients on a monthly retainer basis instead of by the hour. He was reluctant at first, but when he spoke with his clients about it, they were happy to make the switch. Sean now has regained his life and increased his income. He also has a beautiful lawn.

2. Project-Based Model. Independent consultants who work on a project basis perform a specific type of work for a set amount of money. Usually they must produce some type of deliverable, such as a new incentive compensation system, a training program, or a report. They submit a detailed proposal, contract, or letter of agreement up front that clearly specifies the work they will perform, the deliverables they will produce, and the fee they will charge.

For example, Ginny Rehberg (ginny@ginnyrehberg.com) provides corporate outplacement, executive coaching, and career counseling services. Most of her work involves helping executives in career transition to identify their career goals and find new jobs. During a typical day, she will meet with three or four executives in her leased office suite.

Many of Ginny's competitors charge on an hourly basis for these services, but Ginny charges by the project. Some people feel the need to meet with her often, while others only occasionally, but either way she charges a set fee at the outset. She meets with her clients as needed. Her business has been very successful, and over the years she has been able to continually increase her fees.

An advantage of this approach is that the clock does not bind the consultant. Instead of focusing on hours, the consultant can focus on the deliverables and the desired results. Another advantage is that experienced consultants who are able to achieve the results for their clients rapidly (i.e., in relatively few hours) are not penalized. Instead, they are motivated to produce results quickly and efficiently for their client without spending unnecessary time just so they can rack up billable hours.

The disadvantage of this approach is that it requires that consultants accurately predict the amount of effort (i.e., time and resources) they are going to have to expend on a project. If they underestimate the amount of time or effort, they will not make as much money as if they had charged by the hour. Another disadvantage is the problem of "scope creep." This is when the project expands beyond the original contract because the client asks for additional work and assumes that this work is included in the contract. Some consultants encounter difficulties when trying to charge extra for the additional work.

Most of the work that I provide to clients is on a project basis. One of the primary services I provide is conducting employee opinion surveys for organizations. My letter of agreement specifies the work I will perform and what deliverables the client will receive. Since I have conducted these types of projects for many years, I am usually able to accurately predict the time and effort I will need to expend. But even if I underestimate the effort, I'm confident that in the long run things will even out. For every project I overestimate, there will be another that I will underestimate. In the end, I will land more projects because I will be able to tell my client up front what it will cost. That will enable them to budget for the project.

Also, since I have conducted this type of work for many years, I rarely encounter scope creep problems. My contracts clearly outline what work I will perform. If there are deviations from the contract, it is easy for me to warn the client ahead of time or just inform them that there will be additional charges.

3. Retainer-Based Model. Independent consultants who work on a retained basis charge a specified amount of money for a set period of time to provide ongoing or as-needed services.

Retainer arrangements take many forms. Some attorneys, for instance, charge ongoing monthly retainers to their clients that allow them to be available to answer certain types of questions or perform certain types of work. Instead of hiring a staff of attorneys, some organizations will hire attorneys with a certain specialty to be available to answer technical questions in the area of their expertise. Over time, these professionals gain insight into the needs and intricacies of their clients' organizations. They are, therefore, often able to provide accurate advice for less money than the organization would pay if they had to hire an attorney each time they had a new question.

Public relations firms often develop annual retainer agreements with their clients that clearly specify the type of work that will be performed during the year. The firm is then able to devote the appropriate staff and resources to the agreed-upon projects.

Some computer consultants have service agreements with their clients. For a monthly fee, the computer consultant is available to answer their questions and immediately solve problems as they arise.

I have an annual retainer relationship with my accounting firm. Each year I sign a contract with them that specifies what tax filings they will complete and what type of advice they will be available to provide. They invoice me five times a year for predetermined amounts. This has enabled the firm to build an infrastructure that supports my needs and the needs of their other clients. I also sleep better at night because I know there is someone I can always call if I have questions, without having to worry about what the advice is going to cost.

For consultants, the advantage of this type of arrangement is that it provides a predictable, steady flow of income. This enables us to invest in office space, equipment, assistants, et cetera. At the same time, it doesn't make us a slave to the clock and therefore provides us with time to market our services and live our lives. Plus, it provides passive income during periods of time when the client does not ask for service.

Retainer relationships have very few disadvantages. One possible disadvantage is that in some cases a consultant might not be able to charge as much for a retainer as he or she would if a similar type of work were performed on a project basis. Another possible disadvantage that consultants need to avoid is scope creep, when the client demands more and more services over and above what has been agreed. Consultants need to carefully specify what work the retainer covers and what it does not.

4. Results-Based Model. In this business model, the consultant's fee is based on the results achieved for the client. For example:

▫   A sales consultant might charge a percentage of the increase in sales his work generates.

▫   A reengineering consultant might charge a percentage of the decrease in the cost of production of a particular product due to improved efficiency of the operation.

□   A purchasing consultant might charge a percentage of the decreased costs of raw materials.

The advantage of this approach is that since the client has little to lose, you can generally charge more to provide this type of service. There is also the opportunity to leverage your time. If you can develop a solution relatively quickly that achieves the desired result, you can achieve a cash windfall.

The disadvantage of the results-based model is that the consultant receives no money at all if the work performed does not produce tangible results. It also needs to be spelled out precisely how much of the increase in sales or decrease in costs is related to the consultant's work. In order to use this approach, the consultant must be fairly certain he or she can achieve the desired results and that the improvement can be measured and directly related to the services provided.

5. Annuity Service Model. This business model is characterized more by the ongoing nature of the work than how the billing takes place. Consultants who operate within an annuity business model provide services that clients need on an ongoing, rather than periodic, basis. If the consultant can establish a successful relationship with the client, he or she is most probably "locked in" as the preferred provider for many years. This enables the consultant to spend less time marketing and more time serving clients.

Consulting actuaries operate under an annuity service model. Organizations that offer pensions to their employees need actuaries to conduct analyses and submit forms to the government throughout the year. Instead of hiring their own actuaries, organizations hire consultants to perform this work. Unless such consultants make their client unhappy for some reason, they will have a continuous source of income for many years. Typically, they charge on an hourly basis, but some charge a retainer or by the project.

Although they are not professional consultants, the firms that take care of your lawn and landscaping operate an annuity business. The grass continues to grow each year, and unless you are unhappy with their service or decide to take care of the lawn yourself, the lawn care service will have continuous income from you for many years.

This is an excellent business model, because it provides a predictable source of ongoing revenue. Some of the largest consulting firms in the world are benefits consulting firms that provide actuarial services (e.g., Watson Wyatt and Towers Perrin). With their predictable revenue streams, these firms can hire junior consultants and leverage their time to earn more profits.

There are very few disadvantages to this type of business model, unless of course clients cease needing the particular service. This has happened to many actuarial consulting firms in the past decade, as organizations have discontinued their pension programs. In this case, however, it would not have mattered which model the consultant was using to get paid for his services.

6. Consulting Firm Model. Selling the services of others is one of the primary methods that any type of business can use to gain leverage. If you sell services to clients at $2,000 per day and pay an employee or subcontractor $1,000 a day to do the work, you have made $1,000 that you can use to support your business and your personal income. To gain this type of leverage, independent consultants can hire full-time, part-time, or temporary employees, or use subcontractors as needed.

The obvious advantages of this approach are that employees can provide support with client work and assist with marketing. They may also be able to expand your offerings to clients by providing expertise that you don't possess.

Two potential drawbacks to becoming a firm rather than a solo practitioner are the cost and management responsibilities of taking on employees. In order to cover the assistance of others, one must be certain that the income from clients will pay for the increased overhead of salaries, benefits, and office space and equipment. If you are someone who became a consultant in order to avoid the responsibility and hassle of managing others, then building a firm to achieve growth may not be right for you.

Some consultants start their business with the idea that once they bring in enough work, they will be able to hire others. This is possible, but changing an ongoing business model may be difficult. Once you get used to doing everything yourself, you may not be able to let go easily. If your goal is to own and manage a consulting firm, it is wiser to begin your business this way, rather than hope it evolves into something different over time.

7. Outsourcer Service Model. Many organizations outsource organizational functions in order to reduce overhead and increase focus on their core competencies. Organizations outsource services such as security, payroll, benefits administration, building maintenance, cafeteria services, computer support, and purchasing to consulting firms that specialize in this type of work and can do it less expensively. This has opened up many possibilities for consulting firms.

Using this approach, IBM was able to transition from a declining hardware product company to a highly profitable computer services company. Organizations hire them to take over their data centers or to provide desktop computer support to office workers.

The advantage of this approach is that the consulting firm becomes an important part of the client's business and is typically able to land long-term contracts. The disadvantage is the danger of the consultant gradually becoming a consultant in name only, and actually operating as an employee. This is especially true if the consultant must frequently work onsite and fully commit to only one client.

8. Product Sales Model. Selling products is another business model that enables independent consultants to gain leverage. If you create a product once and sell it for the rest of your life, you will continue to earn money from your initial investments of time and energy. Although many consultants use this approach to supplement income, it can be used as your primary or sole business model.

My cowriter, Adam Snyder (www.rembrandtfilms.com), sells DVDs from his website of the animated cartoons his company produces. Visitors to the site can view clips of the cartoons and purchase them using a credit card. The products he sells tend to have a long shelf life, allowing him the potential of receiving this relatively passive income long after he retires.

Rick Brenner of Chaco Canyon Consulting (www.chacocanyon.com) has significantly increased his consulting revenue by selling products on his website. As a consultant, speaker, and coach, he offers his expertise in organizational politics, group dynamics, and unexpected dramatic change, to people at all types of organizations. He writes extensively on these topics in an electronic newsletter he produces weekly and on his website. He uses the newsletter to promote his products, which include tip booklets and e-books.

Developing products with a long shelf life that produce passive income for the foreseeable future can be accomplished on your own schedule. The only possible disadvantage of this approach is that a great deal of uncompensated time may be required to develop the products, as well as market and distribute them.

9. Razor Blade Consulting Sales Model. Manufacturers like Gillette and Schick use a razor blade business model. They sell the handle for their razors relatively inexpensively but charge a substantial amount for the razor blades that consumers must buy on a continuous basis. Companies like Epson and Hewlett-Packard use a similar strategy with their printers. They virtually give away the printer so that you will buy their expensive ink cartridges throughout the year.

This business model is envied by many organizations. It virtually guarantees repeat business and high profits. Can independent consultants develop such a strategy for their businesses? Here is one example.

My Webmaster Ken Hablow (www.KHGraphics.com) creates websites ("razors") for all types of organizations at a modest cost. In addition to the website development charge, he provides ongoing service and support for a monthly fee. Many of his clients use him for this additional service because they don't have the html or design skills he possesses to continually add content and improve the site. Since he developed the site, he has intimate knowledge of its structure and navigation. He is, therefore, the ideal person to provide the "blades."

10. Subscription Model. This business model involves publishing valuable information and selling subscriptions to the information.

The Motley Fool, founded in 1993 by David and Tom Gardner, is a multimedia financial services organization that provides financial investment information. In addition to their free publications, they also charge subscription fees for "premium service" newsletters. A visit to www.fool.com might give you some ideas about how to adopt this type of business model for your consulting business.

Consulting firms that provide highly profitable subscription services to salary compensation data are another example of this model. Human resource managers need to know how the salaries they pay their workers compare to the salaries paid by other organizations for similar workers. This has provided an opportunity for consultants to conduct annual compensation surveys and then charge a subscription fee to organizations that want to purchase a report of the results. Salary surveys are questionnaires sent to human resource managers that simply ask what they pay for each job in their organization. Typically, participating in the survey is a requirement to be able to subscribe to the reporting service. Some of these firms charge companies to participate in the survey and then charge them again for the report.

If you are a specialist in your field, you might be able to develop a subscription service of your own. For instance, if you are a sales consultant, you could provide subscriptions to a publication about sales techniques. If you are a nutrition consultant, you could provide a subscription to a publication that offers nutritional advice.

In addition to the subscription revenue you receive from the publications, you can use the publication as a platform to market your consulting services. You might also be able to attract sponsors and advertising revenue.

This is a way to leverage your content. Publish one issue and then sell it to many people. Only the number of subscriptions you can sell limits the income potential.

Since so much information is available for free on the Web, your information needs to be unique, focused, and packaged in a usable format.

11. Distributor Consulting Model. Another approach to consulting is to become a distributor of consulting products and services that have been developed by others.

This is a relatively quick way to become an independent consultant. Many firms who have developed excellent assessment tools, training programs, and online learning programs certify other professionals to resell their materials. In essence, as the manufacturers of the materials, they rely on independent consultants to distribute their products. Independent consultants purchase the materials from the publisher wholesale and then resell them to their clients at retail prices. They also deliver related support services. Some publishers require an up-front investment for training, certification, or licensing, and some allow you to purchase exclusive rights to a sales territory.

Richard Gaudette of Double Eagle Communications (www. doubleeaglecomm.com) is a training and development consultant who uses the materials of Inscape Publishing. Inscape produces the popular DiSC assessment tool and a variety of training programs for supervisors and managers that Richard uses in his consulting work. He is a distributor for the Inscape products.

The advantage of this model is that the consultant does not incur the costs of developing the tools or programs. The only expense is a licensing or certification fee. The consultant marks up the cost of the products and charges an additional consulting fee for interpreting and implementing them.

One disadvantage of this model is that you don't own the products. You can't claim them as your own or tout yourself as the expert who developed them. Another disadvantage is that the publisher may exert some control on how you use the materials.

12. Publisher Consulting Model. The flip side of the previous model is for you to be the publisher of assessment, training, and other tools and then certify, license, and resell them to others.

This model enables you to leverage the selling efforts of other consultants. You become the manufacturer of intellectual content who achieves a profit from sales made by others. Instead of consulting directly with organizations or individuals, you rely on others to distribute and deliver your materials.

In addition to developing unique, valuable materials, the challenge, of course, is to find consultants who are interested in becoming your distributors. You will need to market your products to them, train them to use the materials, and provide them with ongoing support.

13. Franchiser Consulting Model. A variation and extension of the publishing model is the franchiser model, in which you develop the methods and materials needed for other consultants to provide services to clients.

Mike Myers works for a local franchise of the Sandler Sales Institute, which provides sales training to business owners and executives. Each franchise owns a specific geographic area where it can market and sell the training programs. In addition to developing the workshop and assessment materials, the Institute also provides training on how to deliver the materials and how to market and sell them. The materials and methods they've developed are effective, so they can command a relatively high franchise fee.

Developing a franchise as a new consultant may be difficult, but is certainly possible. You may have experience working as an employee in a situation in which not only do you know how to sell and deliver a particular type of consulting service, you also know exactly how to train others to do so as well. If that's the case, then this could be a good model for you.

The advantage is that you don't have to market, sell, or deliver services to clients. You gain leverage from the fact that you sell the same package to multiple people. Only the number of the franchises you sell to limits your income. Your challenge is to develop the materials and methods (at your expense) and then market and sell the package to franchisees.

14. Franchisee Model. The flip side of the franchiser model is the franchisee model. Here, you as the consultant purchase the franchise. Your job is to market, sell, and deliver the services as specified by the franchiser.

With this model, you don't have to develop the materials or the methods; you just have to implement them. You'll also likely be using methods that have proven effective. The difficulty is that many franchisers charge a high initial fee, as well as annual renewals.

15. Strategic Relationship Model. This model involves establishing a relationship with another consultant or firm so that you provide services to clients together, or they provide you with referrals to their existing client database.

Earlier in my consulting career, I formed a strategic alliance with the consulting firm, Drake Inglesi Milardo, Inc. (www.dimihr.com). This small firm provides a variety of human resource consulting services to organizations in Southern Maine. They needed someone with employee survey expertise to provide services to their clients. My then-fledgling independent consultancy was based in Massachusetts, close enough to their clients for me to drive but far enough away that serving them didn't conflict with the independent identity I had established in Massachusetts. Drake provided me with valuable leads, I provided the services their clients needed, and we shared in the revenue. This strategic relationship was profitable for me for many years.

The advantage of this approach is that the other consultant or firm may be able to provide you with leads and expertise you do not possess. If you can develop a good working relationship and increase the total value provided to the clients, this model can work very well.

However, there are some pitfalls to watch out for before developing a strategic relationship. First, you need to be certain that one plus one equals more than two. Your partner has to provide you with something tangible that has value to your business. Otherwise it is not worthwhile to you, your partner, or the client. I have seen many strategic relationships fail because two independent consultants want company and emotional support, but there is no practical reason for them to work together.

Second, it is important that the relationship doesn't sabotage your own marketing efforts by diluting your identity as an independent consultant. The last thing you want to do is confuse potential clients about who you are and what you do.

Third, there may not be enough revenue to go around. If both you and your strategic partner are going to profit from the relationship, together you have to be able to provide enough value and, therefore, charge enough in fees so that you can both profit.

A final disadvantage of strategic partnerships is that they rarely last. Your needs and the needs of your partners and clients will change over time.

16. General Contractor Model. This model involves developing a relationship with the client and then managing the work of subcontractors who perform the work. The general contractor's responsibilities are to forge the relationship with the client, hire and pay the appropriate subcontractors, supervise their work, and charge the client. In its extreme form, this kind of consultant would not perform any of the actual client work.

You could use this model in your own consulting company. Let's say you were a manager of a computer repair department and you wanted to go into business for yourself, even though you hadn't actually worked on computers for several years. All you would have to do to launch a business using the general contractor model is to be familiar with a few qualified people who could do the work and were willing to work for you as a subcontractor. You would also have to be enthusiastic about marketing this type of independent business on your own.

This approach requires you to manage, rather than perform, the work. If you don't like to manage others, a general contractor model is not for you. It does give you a great deal of leverage, though. You can make money while other people do the work. Another advantage is that it enables you to focus your efforts on marketing and selling rather than time-consuming service delivery.

17. Subcontractor Model. The corollary to the general contractor model is the subcontractor model. Some subcontractors simply subcontract their services to others, who take care of all the marketing and billing tasks. You provide the services and receive a fee, either by the hour or the project.

This is the model I used when I first started my business. I was young and relatively inexperienced, but my college teaching schedule afforded me a good deal of free time. I was able to forge subcontracting relationships with several firms. For one I conducted training programs they had developed; for another I worked on project teams to help their clients identify new products to manufacture; and for a third I developed personnel selection assessments.

For several years this model was ideal for me. I was eventually able to bill out all my available days. I received a great deal of repeat business from the general contractors because they liked my work and made a good profit from my labors.

However, there were a number of problems with the approach. There was a limit to how much I could charge. In order for my client to make a good profit, my rates had to be kept significantly below what they were charging. It was, therefore, difficult for me to increase my income. A second problem was that the clients were not mine. In my efforts to sell my own services directly to clients, I could not ethically use them as references or even get testimonials from them. I certainly couldn't treat them as my own clients. Most importantly, I wasn't building anything. Although I had developed goodwill among the general contractors, I hadn't developed a reputation on my own in the marketplace.

18. Freemium Model. Venture capitalist Fred Wilson in 2006 was the first to describe what he called "the freemium" model in his blog,[2] whereby a consultant gives away services in order to develop a customer base and then begins to offer premium-priced, value-added services to those same customers.

A good example of this model is the telephone company Skype, founded in 2003 by Niklas Zennström and Janus Friis. Based in Luxembourg, Skype gives away its VOIP software as a download from its website. The software allows anyone in the world to make a telephone call to anyone else with the same software installed. Skype generates revenue by charging for premium offerings such as voicemail and call forwarding and for making calls to phones not connected to the Skype software.

Another example is SurveyMonkey, also a Web-based company. They provide a free tool for conducting surveys. They charge only for their premium versions of the service, which include unlimited use of the tool, unlimited number of questions per survey, and more comprehensive e-mail support. These premium offerings are valuable to anyone who frequently conducts surveys, and the price is a relatively modest annual subscription fee.

The advantage of this model is that it enables you to acquire a large number of paying prospects. It also capitalizes on the viral marketing that takes place for free on the Web. If your service is good

---

[2] Musings of a VC in NYC. Fred Wilson's blog: http://www.avc.com/a_vc/2006/03/my_favorite_bus.html.

enough, word travels quickly, and if the premium service is of additional added value, you can profit greatly. The major disadvantage is that you need to create the service initially without a stream of revenue.

Think about the services you provide your clients and try to come up with something very specific you might give away for free, with the expectation that it will introduce you to potential paying clients.

19. Association Model. I know people who have used their expertise in their industries to start their own professional association. They create revenue streams by charging for membership, for attendance at workshops and seminars, for advertising in their newsletter and website, and for enlisting the financial support of sponsors.

Margie Dana left a corporate job where she was in charge of selecting the company's printing vendors. She used the project-based consulting model to start her own business, providing the same type of services. She noticed that there was no place where her prospects, clients, and print vendors could network, share ideas, and learn from each other. She started Print Buyers International (www.printbuyersinternational.com), a professional association catering to those who work in the printing industry (i.e., print buyers, graphic designers, marketing managers, and purchasing executives). She created regular membership events, a newsletter, and online information, all of which she provided free to members. Her income stream comes from membership fees, sponsors, and sales of industry-related products. She also charges for a certification program she has developed.

The best thing about the association model is that you become the go-to person and authority in your field. You can stay at the cutting edge of developments and get to know all the major players.

One disadvantage of this model is that it requires you to manage others. If you are uncomfortable managing, this model may not be the best for you. Another disadvantage is that operating a professional association may preclude you from providing services to clients, since it could represent a conflict of interest. For example, several years ago when I was serving as president of The Society of

Professional Consultants, it would have been a conflict for me to charge for providing mentoring services to consultants. As president, that was part of my job. Members paid their annual dues to the association to be part of a group that mutually supported each other as independent consultants.

20. Speaking Model. This model involves delivering speeches for pay. Organizations and professional associations regularly hire speakers for their company meetings. They look for people to speak on a multitude of topics, including customer service, leadership, innovation, negotiation sales, and personal development. Some are primarily motivational speakers who talk about achieving personal goals or overcoming challenges. Others provide technical training in such areas as computers, financial planning, or taxation.

Most professional speakers also sell consulting services, as well as products such as books, manuals, audio books, and DVDs they can sell to their audiences. Others derive the majority of their income from their speaking fees.

Speaker fees vary greatly but can be quite lucrative. Professional athletes, politicians, and actors can often command tens of thousands of dollars, although most professional speakers charge far less. Some speakers use Speaker's Bureaus to help them recruit clients. You might find it advantageous to do the marketing and negotiate fees with the meeting planners yourself, however.

Many relish the prospect of traveling the world to impart their wisdom or inspirational words. This approach to consulting has many challenges. It can be difficult to find new business, particularly if you are not a celebrity or a well-known authority. Most successful professional speakers have published books in their field. Most also provide consulting services and sell products to supplement their income. When they are not presenting, they must spend a great deal of time marketing. You will also, of course, need to be an excellent presenter on topics that have wide appeal.

21. Public Seminar Model. Public seminars are events where people pay to hear a speaker or attend a seminar. This business model involves marketing the event to potential participants, renting a meeting hall, preparing seminar materials, and conducting the seminar. This is the primary business model for some consultants and consulting firms.

Like me, you probably regularly receive invitations to a variety of seminars on such subjects as time management, managing difficult employees, and getting rich by investing in real estate. This is a challenging business model because the bulk of the work is administrative. There is a great deal of cost and labor involved in procuring mailing lists, designing and mailing invitations, securing the meeting hall, registering attendees, and preparing workshop materials. Standing up and delivering the seminar is the easy part.

22. Author Model. Wouldn't it be nice to just spend your days writing on a topic you love with an occasional call to your publisher and visit to the bank to deposit your royalty checks? It certainly would, but contrary to popular belief, most authors don't receive much money for their books. For example, I will receive only a dollar or two for the sale of this book to you, assuming you bought it retail. Very few business books sell more than five thousand copies.

Solutions

Which consulting model is best for your business? Some general principles follow to guide your decision.

Whichever Consulting Model You Choose, Seek Leverage

Leverage enables you to multiply your effort to produce exponential results. The consulting models that best enable you to gain leverage through the work of employees are the consulting firm, publisher, franchiser, and general contractor models.

With the product sales, franchiser, subscription, freemium, and author models, you can multiply the return on your work by developing products or services in advance and then reselling them.

The annuity, outsourcer, razor blade, and publisher models allow you to leverage your marketing efforts, because once you make one sale, you can have many repeat sales from the same client.

Also, the results-based model provides leverage because, priced appropriately, it can yield a far greater monetary return for your efforts than other consulting models.

Be Clear About Whether or Not You Want to Manage Others

If you enjoy or don't mind managing others, choose from the consulting firm, general contractor, franchiser, or distributor models. If managing others is not your cup of tea, then the time-based, project-based, distributor, franchisee, subcontractor, speaking, or author models may better suit you.

Be Aware of Your Time Horizon

Some consultants need to start earning money immediately and don't have the time or capital to support the up-front development of products or services. In this case, avoid models that require an extended startup period, such as the distributor, franchiser, and freemium models. Models that can yield returns more quickly include the time-based, project-based, distributor, franchisee, strategic relationship, subcontractor, and speaking models.

Consider the Mix You Desire for Marketing and Delivering Services

The models that yield a high level of repeat business generally necessitate less marketing than other models. They include the time-based, retainer-based, annuity, outsourcer, and subcontractor models.

Ponder the Possibility of Passive Income

If you are excited about the idea of receiving passive income, consider the retainer-based, consulting firm, product sales, razor blade, distributor, franchiser, general contractor, freemium, subscription, association, author, and publisher models.

Think About Your Desire for Income

All the consulting models described above have the potential for producing a high level of income. Models with the greatest potential for producing high income are the retainer-based, results-based, distributor, annuity, consulting firm, publisher, franchiser, and general contractor models.

Bear in Mind Your Desire for Work/Life Balance

The consulting models offering the least potential for good work/life balance are the time-based, outsourcer, strategic relationship, subcontractor, speaking, and public seminar models.

Conclusion

It is important at the outset of your business to understand the advantages and disadvantages of each business model. You need to assess whether the model you select has the potential to provide you with the work/life balance you desire and to enable you to meet your goals for personal growth and income.

Even after you have established your consulting business, you need to periodically step back and take an objective view of the business model you are using and ask yourself whether it is working for you. Try to imagine using a different model. If you are not achieving your goals, consider a fundamental change.

CHAPTER 5

Establishing Your Credibility

AURIE CAME TO MY OFFICE in need of assistance. She was an accomplished technology business strategist with a great deal of in-house company experience managing computerized information systems. Since leaving her last job, she had been working as a subcontractor for a small consulting firm in her field. Now that she had a taste of consulting, she liked it, and she wanted to find her own clients, but she was a novice as a consultant. She needed to quickly establish her credibility as an expert in her field.

Roberta Matuson is president of Human Resource Solutions (www.yourhrexperts.com) and an independent consultant who has been in business for more than twelve years. After ten years she realized that she needed to branch out. She looked out at the horizon and noted that organizations were struggling with the issues of recruiting, managing, and retaining Generation Y employees. She needed to position herself as an expert on the topic of helping organizations leverage their intergenerational workforce challenges into opportunities.

The Challenge

Although they know they can do the work and do it well, many beginning consultants are often concerned they won't appear credible to prospects. They worry that they:

◻ **Do not have a proven track record as a consultant.** Beginning consultants feel intimidated if they do not have a long client list or testimonials from satisfied Fortune 500 clients. They believe that their expertise and success as employees will be discounted by prospects. It is more important for you to stress your confidence that you can solve organizational problems.

◻ **Did not graduate with an advanced degree from an Ivy League college.** While some prospects are impressed by pedigrees, most are focused primarily on whether you can solve their problem. Many are actually turned off by advanced degrees, preferring business experience to academic success.

◻ **Do not have glitzy marketing materials like many competitors.** They worry that they don't have four-color glossy brochures or a website filled with information about their work. But prospects are more impressed by your ideas, your approach, and how you present yourself when you meet them.

◻ **Do not have a national reputation.** Many are also concerned that prospects won't take them seriously because they have not yet made a name for themselves in their field. Again, your ideas and approach are more important than your reputation. Most prospects don't even know the names of the leading experts in your field, and not everyone expects to hire the nation's lead expert to solve their problems. They want someone who is committed to listening to them and understanding their situation.

Solutions

Although you may not have established a consulting track record yet in your field, you *are* an expert, and you need to be able to appear that way to prospects. Establishing your credibility requires a disciplined and sustained marketing campaign. We will discuss the various marketing approaches in detail in later chapters, but here are some basic strategies for initially establishing your credibility in the marketplace.

Send Out a Formal Announcement

The first step is to let the people with whom you have already established credibility know about your business. Put a stake in the ground and tell the world that you have launched a consulting business and this is how you can be reached.

Start with your current network. These people are your most likely source of clients. Your network includes everyone you know (e.g., your professional contacts, colleagues, coworkers, former coworkers, friends, relatives, neighbors, and acquaintances). Some of these people know the quality of your work, and probably most of them like you and want you to succeed in your business. Don't artificially limit the list. You never know who can help you. My first piece of business as a consultant came from a lead from my long-retired mother-in-law.

If you do not have lists of current mail and e-mail addresses for your network, get busy assembling them. Your network is one of the most important business assets you possess, even more important than your professional skills. Do it quickly. You have bills to pay.

Go to a printer and have them print up a nice formal announcement card for you. It needs to look professional. If you have the funds, work with a designer to help you choose the style, fonts, and appearance. A designer can also help you create a logo for your business.

The announcement should contain your company name, logo (if you have one), and contact information. Most importantly, it should state the type of business you are conducting and the kind of results you are going to provide to clients.

For example, when I started my consulting business in 1993, I sent the following formal printed announcement to everyone in my address book:

Bruce Katcher is pleased to announce the founding of The Discovery Consulting Group. We specialize in helping organizations gain a better understanding of how their employees and customers really feel about them.

Be sure to order matching envelopes. Hand addressing and

stamping, although more work, will increase the likelihood that the envelope will be opened. In addition, be sure to include your return address so that the recipient will see right away that it is from you.

You might also send a similar announcement via e-mail. Keep it short. Most people do not like to read long e-mails, even from a good friend.

Collect Testimonials

Testimonials are an excellent method for establishing your credibility. Positive words about your work from a client or a recognizable source can have a great impact on your prospects. Testimonials actually transfer the credibility of others and their organization to you.

Undoubtedly, there are people in your professional network who would be willing to testify to the quality of your work. You need to get them to do so in writing. They don't need to be former clients. They can be former coworkers, managers, or satisfied customers from jobs you have held.

A testimonial should be short and to the point. Ask people who know your work to write a few words about you that you can use in your marketing. Encourage them to state how you helped them. Ideally, people or organizations whose names your prospects will recognize should write your testimonials. Here are a few examples of mine.

Although it is a small firm, Discovery Surveys shows remarkable flexibility, innovation, and ability to meet tight deadlines. The help in communicating the most important results to management and employees has been exceptional. I'll continue to use Discovery Surveys for any employee survey work—focus groups to paper and pencil or Internet.

FRANCES GALLITANO
VICE PRESIDENT OF HUMAN RESOURCES
DELTA DENTAL PLAN OF MASSACHUSETTS

Discovery Surveys has conducted several employee surveys for our organization. They have been very flexible and responsive to our needs. We were particularly pleased with their creative solutions for communicating the results to employees, and the quality of their suggestions for addressing the issues identified via the survey.

Michael N. Piergrossi
Vice President of Human Resources and Organizational Development
W.R. Grace

Bruce's presentation kicked off our program year on a high note. Members commented that they enjoyed his program and found his practical advice and commonsense approach valuable. Bruce left us with tips that we could take back to the office and use that day.

Ms. Lynn P. Watterson, SPHR
President
Human Resources Management Association of Rhode Island

Use your testimonials as frequently as possible. Create a one-page listing of them and include it in your proposals and your press kit. Post your testimonials on your website and print them in your brochure and possibly even on your business card. They are powerful.

Obtain Referrals

A referral to a qualified prospect from a satisfied client is the most powerful method for establishing credibility.

Don't be passive about referrals. Don't just assume that people who are satisfied with your work will tell others about you. You have to ask satisfied clients, previous employers, and respected colleagues if they would be willing to tell others about the value you provide.

There are three types of referrals: hot, warm, and cold. The most useful referral is a hot referral. This is when a satisfied client contacts a prospect on your behalf to tell them about the quality of your work and then either has the prospect contact you or calls to tell you that the prospect is interested and awaiting your call.

A warm referral is when your satisfied client tells you about a prospect you should contact and gives you permission to use his or her name when you contact them. This is certainly useful, but not as useful as a hot referral.

A cold referral is when a satisfied client mentions a person you should call but doesn't know the person or doesn't want you to use his or her name as a reference. This type of referral is the most difficult to convert into a meeting, but by all means, follow through and try to contact the prospect. Nothing ventured, nothing gained.

Conduct an Endorsement Campaign

An endorsement is a supercharged testimonial. Just like referrals and testimonials, endorsements transfer the credibility of someone else directly to you. Actors, actresses, and professional athletes are paid a great deal of money to endorse products and services. The reason: The approach works. You can make it work for you as well, and you don't need to pay a celebrity. Here is the basic approach:

Step 1: Obtain the cooperation of the endorser. For the approach to be successful, this person should be a known and respected authority in your field.

Step 2: Ask your endorser to write a letter on their letterhead about you and the quality of your work. Offer to write the letter for them, or hire a marketing consultant to write it.

Step 3: Develop a list of prospects. Ideally, these will be people that your endorser knows, but that is not necessary. In any case, the prospects should be people who know and respect your endorser.

Step 4: Send the letter from your endorser to the prospects.

Step 5: Follow up with one or two of your own letters or a phone call, making certain to mention the initial letter from your endorser.

Bob Martel of JMB Marketing (BobMartel@jmbmarketing.com) is a marketing consultant who specializes in helping his clients conduct endorsement campaigns. Several years ago he helped Jan Stanley, a marketing consultant who had just completed a consulting project for a well-known CEO of a Fortune 500 retailer. Bob wrote the letter, and Jan had the CEO sign it and provide a stack of his letterhead. The letter talked about the great work that Jan had provided to the company and suggested recipients contact her for similar marketing assistance. Jan and Bob sent the letter to sixty-six CEOs of noncompeting Fortune 500 firms. The endorsement changed the sales dynamic for Jan, and she landed several new clients as a direct result of this campaign.

Conclusion

The key to establishing your credibility in the early stages of your consulting business is to leverage the credibility of others. Testimonials, referrals, and endorsements are effective methods for transferring the trust that others have in you to your prospects.

Other approaches for establishing your credibility as your business unfolds are writing articles, delivering speeches, writing books, conducting original research, and appearing on radio and television. These will be discussed in later chapters.

It takes planning and perspiration, but you can quickly establish your credibility in the marketplace.

PART 2

Marketing Your
Consulting Services

CHAPTER 6

Developing and Implementing a Marketing Plan

M Y COUSIN'S WIFE, Peri Basel, has a unique type of consulting
practice. Her firm helps cosmetic plastic surgeons and their office
staff better market their services to potential patients (www.cosmet-
icphysiciansolutions.com).

Prior to beginning her own business, Peri had amassed a successful track record of improving business for several cosmetic plastic surgeons while she worked for them as an employee. She developed websites, discovered press opportunities with the local newspapers, radio and television stations, and helped them to focus their
business on more lucrative procedures. She also trained the office
staff how to more efficiently run the office, identify the best patient
prospects, and successfully close sales.

But working every day in an office and dealing with the internal
office politics had become a grind. She had also been laid off several
times when the physicians she worked for decided they couldn't
afford a full-time marketing person. She decided to offer the same

services to physicians as an independent consultant. That would eliminate her daily commute, provide her more control of her time, and potentially lead to more income.

Peri was confident she could make the business work. She had achieved many tangible positive outcomes (i.e., both increased income and reduced expenses) for physicians in the past and had gathered many glowing testimonials from well-known physicians in her area.

The dilemma she faced was how to get the word out to other cosmetic plastic surgeons so that they would use her services. She had to overcome a number of challenges:

◻ Physicians don't like to spend money for consulting services. They are accustomed to hiring relatively low-paid receptionists, clerical staff, and office managers and having them work on marketing as well.

◻ The economy was in a recession, and although physicians desperately needed to increase business, many felt that they were not in a position to invest in marketing.

◻ Physicians are very busy during the workday and usually don't answer their own phones or even open their mail. It was difficult to get their attention.

◻ She had limited financial resources to invest in marketing her own business.

The Challenge

Getting the word out, or marketing, is a challenge most consultants face, especially those just starting a consulting practice. Marketing includes everything that you do to promote yourself and your services, and it is something that needs to become part of who you are and what you do every day.

Successful consultants realize that there are only three types of people in their world: clients, prospects, and those who can lead you to prospects. Your antennae always need to be extended and on the lookout for new business. Your next client can be someone you meet at a professional meeting, your neighbor, someone you used to work with twenty years ago, or even someone you sit next to on an airplane. For example, my most recent clients are people who read my book, saw my electronic newsletter on someone else's website, heard a speech I had delivered, saw an advertisement I had placed in a local trade publication, or have been referred from a fellow consultant.

There are undoubtedly many other consultants who have the same level of technical skills and professional experience as you. But skills and experience in your field are only a small part of why you will succeed or fail as an independent consultant. Those who can market successfully will succeed. Those who don't are destined to fail. Marketing has to be something you embrace as a welcome challenge rather than a necessary evil. Show me a consultant who does no marketing and I'll show you a soon-to-be ex-consultant.

You may hear from some established consultants that they don't do any marketing because all of their business comes by referral. What they fail to realize, however, is that they really *are* marketing. Although they may not be conducting cold calls or direct mail campaigns, they are attending professional meetings, maintaining contact with their network, and entertaining prospects. These are very important marketing techniques that lead to referrals.

Part II of this book will cover eighteen ways to market your consulting business, all of which are listed in Table 6-1, which also compares each approach using seven criteria.

As you look at the list, you might think, "Some of these approaches are effective and others are not." You would be wrong. Conducted properly, every one of the marketing techniques I will describe can lead to a wealth of new business for independent consultants.

You might also think, "Some of the approaches could never work for the type of consulting service that I provide." You would be wrong again. Every one of these techniques can be effective, no matter what type of consulting service you provide. Again, the key is to conduct them properly.

There are seven criteria for evaluating the different marketing techniques available to you in starting and growing your consulting practice:

TABLE 6-1. EIGHTEEN APPROACHES TO MARKETING CONSULTING SERVICES EVALUATED USING SEVEN CRITERIA.

MARKETING APPROACH	Cost	Time Commitment	Time Horizon	Ease of Delegating	Writing Skills Needed	Presentation Skills Needed	Interpersonal Skills Needed
Direct Approaches:							
1. Direct Mail	High	Med	Short	High	Med	Low	Low
2. Direct E-mail	Low	Med	Short	Med	High	Low	Low
3. Cold Calls	Low	Med	Short	High	Low	Low	High
Writing:							
4. White Papers	Low	Med	Long	Low	High	Low	Low
5. Articles	Low	Med	Long	Low	High	Low	Low
6. Books	Low	High	Long	Low	High	Low	Low
7. Newsletter	High	High	Long	Med	High	Low	Low
8. Electronic Newsletter	Low	Med	Long	Low	High	Low	Low
9. Blog	Low	Med	Long	Low	High	Low	Low
Speaking:							
10. Speeches	Low	Med	Med	Low	Low	High	High
11. Teach a Course	Low	High	Med	Low	Low	High	High
Maintaining Visibility:							
12. A Website	High	Med	Long	Med	Med	Low	Low
13. Advertise	High	Low	Med	High	Med	Low	Low
14. Press Releases	Low	Med	Long	High	High	Low	Low
15. Radio and TV Interviews	Low	Low	Long	Low	Low	High	High
Networking:							
16. Contact with Your Network	Low	Med	Short	Low	Low	Low	High
17. Relationships with Service Providers	Low	Low	Med	Low	Low	Low	High
18. Professional Meetings	Med	Med	Long	Low	Low	Low	High

1. **Cost:** Do you have a startup budget to support your marketing efforts? Many of the approaches require very little, if any, money, but some involve out-of-pocket costs for printing, postage, telephone, Internet access, meeting registration fees, advertising fees, purchase of mail lists, and travel.

2. **Time Commitment:** Do you have time available in your schedule to devote to marketing? Some of the marketing approaches are time consuming, while others require relatively little time. Which techniques you use may be limited by the consulting business model you are using. For example, if you are using the time-based consulting model, you will probably have very little time available in your workweek to conduct cold calls or write a book.

3. **Time Horizon:** Do you need business immediately, or can you invest time in building your brand in the marketplace? Conducted properly, some of the marketing approaches, such as keeping up with your network, cold calls, and direct mail, can relatively quickly lead to business. Most of the approaches, however, will produce results only in the long term. For example, advertising, articles in trade publications, and books all help you to establish your professional image in the marketplace but rarely lead to instant new business.

4. **Ease of Delegating:** Do you want to try to delegate your marketing activities to others or conduct it all yourself? Some of the marketing techniques, such as cold calling, direct mail, and writing press releases, can be delegated to employees, virtual assistants, marketing consultants, or subcontractors. Others, such as delivering speeches, writing a blog, teaching a course, and attending professional meetings, cannot be delegated.

5. **Writing Skills:** Are you a good writer? Strong writing skills are necessary for marketing activities such as publishing articles and books, writing newsletters, and publishing a blog. Other approaches require little or no writing skills.

6. **Presentation Skills:** Do you have strong presentation skills? Standing in front of a group to deliver a speech is not everyone's cup of tea. Fear not. Most of the basic approaches to marketing do not require this skill.

7. **Interpersonal Skills:** Do you have strong interpersonal commu-

nication skills? Some marketing approaches, such as cold calling, maintaining contact with your network, and developing relationships with service providers, require a high level of interpersonal skills. Approaches such as advertising, direct mail, and publishing do not.

Solutions

Here are ten general strategies to guide your decisions about which marketing approaches are best for your business.

Develop a Marketing Strategy

Once or twice a year, ask yourself three basic questions:

1. What needs in the marketplace can I meet?
2. What markets am I going to target that have that need?
3. How am I going to reach those target markets?

Armed with the answers to these questions, you will be able to ask yourself further questions that will guide your marketing plans, such as:

- What type of direct marketing approaches will I implement?
- What will I write and speak about?
- How will I maintain my visibility in the marketplace?
- Where and how will I network?

Earmark Funds for Marketing

Marketing is the key to keeping your business surviving and thriving. As in any business, you need to make certain that you earmark funds for marketing. You will need funding for stationery, postage, printing, website maintenance, advertising, and attending networking meetings.

As shown in Table 6-1, even if your funds are limited there are some marketing activities you can conduct for virtually no financial investment, such as cold calling, writing papers and articles, publishing an electronic newsletter or blog, maintaining contact with your network, and developing relationships with other professional service providers.

Don't Be Afraid to Outsource When Necessary

You need to understand what you can and cannot do well. For example, if you don't have the inclination or aptitude to learn html, then hire a Webmaster to create and maintain your site. If you are not a great writer, then hire an editor.

Be Consistent

Regardless of the specific approach you use, you must market on a consistent basis. Publishing an electronic newsletter every six months will not be nearly as effective as producing one monthly. Attending professional association meetings periodically will not be nearly as useful as attending them regularly.

Most importantly, marketing only when business is slow is a recipe for disaster. Many approaches, such as speaking, publishing, advertising, and attending professional meetings, have impact only in the long term. You must, therefore, make certain that you reserve time and that these activities occur regularly, even when you are busy consulting with clients.

Develop schedules, timelines, and deadlines for yourself for writing papers, publishing newsletters, and launching mail campaigns. If you leave these activities to chance, they won't happen consistently enough to lead to new business.

Use a Combination of Approaches

Some prospects are motivated to take action in response to mailings or phone calls. Others are more likely to respond to written articles or speeches. Still others scan the Web or directories when they have a need. You will, therefore, need to use a variety of approaches to cast a wide net to reach these various types of prospects. Ideally, you will use a combination of both direct (i.e., direct mailing and cold calling) and indirect (i.e., writing, speaking, advertising, and networking) approaches toward maintaining your visibility.

Focus Your Marketing Efforts

While using a combination of marketing approaches is important, it is better to use one approach very well than many approaches halfheartedly. If you are a good speaker and have found that it leads to new clients, do it often, not occasionally. If your experience tells you that writing articles leads to new business, create a goal for yourself of publishing, say, an article every month, and stick to it.

Use Marketing Approaches You Enjoy

If you dislike speaking in front of an audience but have found other marketing approaches that work for you, then stick to those that you enjoy. Life is too short to spend time doing things you dislike. Besides, if you don't like doing it, you won't do it consistently, and you likely won't be good at it.

Develop a Detailed Marketing Implementation Plan

Most consultants have in mind plenty of marketing activities they are planning to conduct but are not systematic about scheduling these activities. Table 6-2 presents part of a marketing plan I have used. The method is not sophisticated or complex, but it is practical and can

Survey Results: Do Consultants Have Written Marketing Plans?

Only about 20 percent of The Consulting 200 have a written marketing plan that they follow.

I currently have a written marketing plan that I follow.

Percent	
20	Strongly agree or agree
30	Partly agree/Partly disagree
50	Disagree or strongly disagree

keep you organized. It's simply a spreadsheet that organizes the major marketing activities you plan on conducting to support your consulting practice. Each row of the spreadsheet contains the planned marketing activities, grouped by service line. The primary service lines I was providing at the time I created this plan were Employee Opinion Surveys (EOS), Customer Satisfaction Surveys (CSS), and Paid Speaking Engagements (PSE). An X in a cell meant that I was going to conduct the activity that month.

TABLE 6-2. A PARTIAL SAMPLE MARKETING PLAN.

GOAL	ACTIVITY	Jan	Feb	March	April	May
EOS	Publish and distribute newsletter to network	X	X	X	X	X
EOS	Publish an article in a trade publication			X		X
EOS	Deliver a pro bono marketing speech		X		X	
EOS	Conduct a survey of HR professionals				X	
CSS	Send a mailing to CEOs and presidents			X		
CSS	Send a mailing to network					X
PSE	Send a mailing to meeting planners				X	
PSE	Produce a sample videotape					X
PSE	Mail a one-pager to network			X		

Become a Student of Marketing

Talk to other consultants about how they are marketing their services. Attend professional meetings where marketing is discussed. Join a professional association of marketers, such as the American Marketing Association. Visit your local bookstore and buy the latest books on marketing approaches.

Evaluate Your Marketing Activities

They say that insanity is doing the same thing over and over again and expecting different results. Periodically you need to systematically evaluate your marketing activities. Think back over the list of clients you have landed during the past six months or year, or think about your best clients. How did they learn about you? Was it through something you wrote, a speech you gave, a mailing you conducted, an advertisement you placed, or a referral from a colleague at a professional meeting?

The answers to these questions should determine which marketing activities you should improve upon or abandon and which you should continue or intensify.

Conclusion

We started this chapter talking about Peri Basel's fledgling consulting practice. She faced several challenges: creating a new type of consulting business, marketing to physicians who don't like to spend money for consultants, trying to launch a business during an economic downturn, and trying to sell to physicians who are usually too busy to even answer their own phones. How did she do it? She used a variety of marketing approaches, including:

- **An e-mail campaign.** Although physicians are difficult to reach by telephone, she knew that many of them did look at their own e-mails. With the assistance of other service providers who serve cosmetic plastic surgeons, she developed an e-mail list of more than a hundred cosmetic plastic surgeons in her area and e-mailed them about her services and how she could help them. The campaign included several e-mail messages and follow-up phone calls.

- **A website.** Peri created an impressive-looking website that described her services and included testimonials from satisfied clients. This was critical, since website creation was part of the service she was offering.

- **The press.** Peri was featured in several local newspaper articles that talked about how women were spending less on cosmetic surgery during the economic downturn. The articles talked about what basic work they were having done to keep them looking young. She then featured these articles on her website.

I am happy to report that at this writing, Peri's marketing has led to several new clients, and her business is thriving. She was able to successfully create a new type of consulting business in a struggling economy by both helping cosmetic physicians to address the downturn in their business and working strategically and tirelessly to market her own business.

Each of the eighteen marketing techniques shown in Table 6-1 is described in more detail in chapters 7 through 11.

CHAPTER 7

Marketing Directly to Prospects

C AN YOU POSSIBLY LAND NEW consulting business by simply sending out a brochure about your services to people you don't know? Absolutely! I have done it many times. Why do you think your mailbox is full of brochures from retailers and service providers? It is one of the many marketing strategies that can work, if conducted properly.

There are many ways to conduct direct e-mail campaigns. Here is a brief description of a few campaigns that have worked for me.

One of the major services I have provided for many years is conducting customized employee opinion surveys. I target senior human resource professionals in organizations with more than 100 employees based in New England. Several years ago, I conducted a simple direct mail campaign that resulted in several new clients.

I first assembled a mailing list. It was a time-consuming task. I purchased a list from a broker and expanded it based on contacts from human resource professional associations in my area. I then placed all of the information in my spreadsheet program. It contained five hundred prospects.

When I started my business, I printed a thousand six-inch by nine-inch tri-folded brochures. The brochures were cleverly designed. My logo is a dark blue four-pane window. The brochure had a large version of this window logo on the front. It opened by opening the window. The inside contained my contact information and some bulleted information about how my services had helped other organizations reduce employee turnover, improve employee morale, and improve employee productivity.

I also printed postcard-size bounceback cards. These cards had my address on the front and a place for a stamp. The back had spaces for my prospects to enter their contact information and a few check boxes asking them if they wanted to be contacted.

I conducted a mail merge with my database and created personalized one-page cover letters. The cover letters were printed on my letterhead and contained the inside address of the prospects. The letter itself discussed briefly how I might be able to help them and contained a short list of my clients. I signed each of the letters, affixed postage on the outer envelope, and placed them in the mail.

Within a few days I started receiving completed bounce back cards. I followed up with these leads and turned several of them into new clients. One year later, I was still receiving a returned card every once in awhile. I was able to turn some of them into new clients as well.

Here is another example of how I have used direct mail, which is also an example of guerilla marketing.

Several years ago I was a member of a national association of public speakers that helps people improve their speaking ability and learn how to market their speaking services. The members speak on every topic imaginable, ranging from managing personal finances to managing employees.

At the meetings of my local chapter, I met many people who spoke on the topic of improving customer service. One of the services I provide is conducting customer satisfaction surveys for organizations that are trying to improve their service to customers. Several of the members said that they would keep me in mind because many of their clients could probably use this service.

One day I received a CD in the mail from the association. It contained a membership directory, locked with a password. The password that they included only allowed me to see my own information to make certain it was correct. It listed my contact information and all of the topics that I present to audiences.

I then had a brainstorm. If I could access all of the information on the disk, I would be able to identify the names and e-mail addresses of members throughout the country who spoke about customer service. I could then conduct an e-mail campaign to these people promoting my customer surveys. The information was already public, published in an annual print directory.

I contacted a computer-savvy buddy of mine and asked him to see if he could unlock the database. He was able to do this easily. The spreadsheet clearly showed the contact information of the hundreds of members who had spoken about improving customer service.

I then created an e-mail message that discussed possible synergy between the customer service work that they conducted and my surveys. I e-mailed it to everyone on the list. Only a handful of speakers e-mailed me back, and none of those were promising leads.

Several weeks later I received an e-mail from an executive from the national headquarters of the association. I felt a pain in the pit of my stomach. I was worried that they were going to chastise me for e-mailing members. With trepidation, I opened the e-mail. It said, "Several members forwarded the e-mail you sent to them about your customer satisfaction survey work." Now I was really worried. Then it said, "It just so happens that we have a need for your services." One thing led to another, and the association became a client.

The moral of this story is that e-mail marketing works. You never know what good things can happen if you spend the time and energy to conduct direct mail campaigns.

The Challenge

Although direct mail can be an effective approach for marketing consulting services, it poses some daunting challenges:

- You are trying to generate interest from people who don't know anything about you and have every reason to be cynical about the value of your services.

◘   It is time consuming. Direct mail campaigns require a great deal of time to plan and execute.

◘   It is labor intensive. Tasks such as assembling or purchasing mailing lists, purchasing stationery, conducting mail merges, signing letters, stuffing envelopes, and affixing postage all require a great deal of effort. These tasks, of course, can be delegated, but that will require your management attention and, perhaps, additional cost.

◘   It can be expensive. The costs of acquiring mailing lists, printing, and postage can all add up. E-mail campaigns are typically less expensive but may also incur costs for mailing lists and, perhaps, e-mail distribution costs if you use a bulk html e-mail service.

Solutions

The three direct marketing techniques of direct mail, direct e-mail, and cold calling are described below.

Direct Mail

Direct mail, direct e-mail, and cold calling are the three most straightforward marketing approaches, allowing you to make contact directly with the prospect. Direct mail involves developing or acquiring a mailing list of prospects and then sending some kind of promotional material to the list.

A direct mail campaign by mail involves these five steps.

Step 1: Plan the campaign. Rather than sending out one letter, plan a sustained mail campaign. One-shot mailings are not as effective as campaigns involving multiple mailings and follow-up phone calls. You will need to make certain you have a good mailing list, ample stationery, and the appropriate enclosures, such as a white paper you have written, a reprint of an article you have bylined, or a brochure. It is also a good idea to include a bounce back card to make it easy for the prospect to contact you. It is also important that you set realistic expectations. Like other marketing approaches, a direct mail campaign is a numbers game. Typically, you can expect only a 1 or 2 percent hit rate. Therefore, the more you send, the greater number of hits.

Step 2: Assemble the mailing list. The quality of the mailing list is the key to a successful direct mail campaign. In other words, you have to be mailing to the right people (i.e., those who are legitimate prospects), and the list needs to be accurate in terms of spelling, contact information, and job titles.

The best list (assuming it is current) is your own database. This is because you already know these people. You are a known quantity to them, and they trust you. That's where you should start.

Once you have exhausted your own mailing list, try to reach out to strangers by acquiring or assembling a mailing list. Assembling a mailing list yourself is time consuming but may be appropriate if you have an unusual or specific target market, no budget, and the necessary time. For example, here are a few of the highly specific mail lists I have created for myself in the past:

◻ Newly appointed vice presidents of human resource professionals

◻ Meeting planners for national management associations

◻ Presidents of biotechnology companies in my geographic area

◻ Human resource professionals in companies identified by my local newspaper as "Best Places to Work"

With a little practice and persistence, most mailing lists can be assembled free by scanning the Web for the names and addresses you are seeking. E-mail addresses are more difficult to find on the Web, but many can be located.

But you certainly don't have to assemble the mail list yourself. There are many services (e.g., Hoover's and InfoUSA) that sell mailing lists. Just search your local Yellow Pages or scan the Web to find companies and list brokers that can sell you very targeted lists. For example:

◻ If you are a financial adviser, you could buy a list of heads of households with annual incomes over $300,000 in the ten zip codes nearest your home.

◻ If you are a quality improvement consultant, you could buy a list of the CEOs, presidents, and vice presidents of purchasing at manufacturing companies in the four states within driving distance of your office.

▫   If you conduct strategic planning for magazine publishers, you could purchase an international list of companies that publish magazines.

List services charge for the number of names you purchase, as well as for the format in which they provide them to you (e.g., print-out, mailing labels, spreadsheet). They typically charge extra for sorting the list by variables such as job title, industry sector, size, and geography.

It will be up to you, however, to be creative concerning the kind of list you ask a list service to create for you. My coauthor, Adam Snyder at www.RembrandtFilms.com, writes corporate histories, among many other kinds of business writing. He has had several privately held clients with long, proud histories that have hired him to document that history in a book, pamphlet, or short documentary. Some have had him produce books or booklets that they then distributed to customers and employees as they celebrated a milestone, such as a major anniversary. Adam was seeking new clients and wanted to reach out to these types of companies. Using a reputable mailing list provider, he was able to purchase a list of the presidents and CEOs of private companies with at least $50 million in sales that during the upcoming year would be celebrating a twenty-fifth-, fiftieth-, seventy-fifth-, or hundredth-year anniversary.

Some mailing list services provide "one-time-use," while others allow you to use the list multiple times in any way you see fit. Some will provide you with labels or an electronic database so that you can create your own labels or use the addresses in any way you like (e.g., as inside addresses on cover letters). Some mailing list services guarantee the accuracy of their lists, and others do not. (Accuracy is typically defined as the percentage of the returns you receive from the post office.)

If you are a member of a professional association, you probably have access to its membership list. Keep in mind, however, that many professional associations frown on members using the membership list for a mailing. This is either to protect their members from being deluged with marketing materials from members, or because they sell the mailing lists themselves.

Step 3: Write a cover letter. The letter needs to be well written and to the point. Use simple, conversational language. Some say you should limit the letter to one page, but length is not important. Some of the most effective sales letters are as long as ten pages or as short as a paragraph. Here are a few key points to keep in mind:

- **It's not about you; it's about your prospect.** The tendency is to write about yourself, your capabilities, and all the wonderful things you have done for your clients. But your prospects are interested in themselves and solving their own problems. Write from the point of view of the benefits to them, not the features of your services.

- **Capture their attention immediately.** The opening paragraph or two of the letter needs to grab the reader's attention by talking about the problems they face. Here are some examples of how a letter might begin:

  From a computer security consultant: "How would you like to stop worrying about losing valuable data?"

  From a financial adviser: "Are you prepared for the next stock market surprise?"

  From an executive coach: "How much would it be worth to your company if you could improve the performance of your weakest senior manager?"

  From a marketing consultant: "Are you wasting your time meeting with prospects who will never purchase your services?"

  From a sales consultant: "Suppose you could sit down today and write a sales letter that would provide you with all of the business you can handle."

- **Remember the objective of the letter.** The purpose of the direct mail marketing letter is not to close the sale. The objective is to get the prospect interested enough to take an action, such as sending back the response card, calling or e-mailing you, or visiting your website.

- **Make it easy to read.** Use short paragraphs, bullets, numbered lists, capitalization, bold font, italics, and lots of white space.

- **Personalize the salutation.** Use their name rather than "Dear Colleague," "Dear Friend," or "To Whom This May Concern." If you use their first name, try to learn their preferred name (e.g., Bill instead of William, Bob instead of Robert, Jim instead of James).

❑ **Personalize the letter.** If at all possible, personalize the letter to include information about the prospect, references to other work you have done for the prospect's organization, someone the prospect knows, or information about their specific problems.

❑ **Use headers and postscripts.** The reader's eye is naturally drawn to the top and the bottom of letters. Consider including a phrase or sentence at the top of the letter (above the date and inside address), as well as a postscript at the end of the letter. These are more likely to be read than the letter itself.

❑ **Include a free offer.** Make it easy for the prospect to make contact with you by offering them things such as a free initial consultation or a free article, subscription to your newsletter, or copy of your book.

❑ **Include a call to action.** Ask your prospects to do something, such as call you using your toll-free number, send back the enclosed reply card, or e-mail you to schedule an appointment.

Step 4: Assemble the mail package. The mail package includes the outer envelope and enclosures (including the cover letter). Here are a few suggestions:

❑ **The outer envelope.** Even the best cover letters go unread in direct mail campaigns that fail to pay attention to the outer envelope. The objective is to get people to open your package. The general rule of thumb is that anything you can do to make the mailing look personal rather than mass-produced will increase the probability that it will be opened. Consider:

Using stamps rather than metered postage

Printing the addresses on the envelope rather than using printed labels

Addressing the envelopes by hand

Using a nonstandard-size envelope

Using a plain envelope rather than one with your company's return address

Writing a key phrase or benefit on the outer envelope

◻   **The enclosures.** In addition to the cover letter, consider including:

> A list of testimonials from satisfied clients
>
> A brochure about your services or a list of problems that you solved for clients
>
> A white paper or reprint of an article you have recently published
>
> A prestamped bounceback card addressed to you (the card should contain space for the prospect to write her or his contact information and check boxes to indicate what they would like to receive from you)

Step 5: Follow up. The initial mailing is only the first step in your direct mail campaign. In the first place, your prospect may discard the mailing without opening it, or an assistant may discard it even before your prospect has the option of deciding whether to open it. Sending additional mailings or following up in other ways may help mitigate these problems. Secondly, most marketing and sales professionals will tell you that in order to close a sale, you need lots of "touches." A touch is any contact you have with a prospect, including mailings, telephone calls, e-mails, and meetings. And thirdly, by following up with additional mailings or other attempts to contact your prospect, you will leverage the work you have already expended to create the mail list or the expense you have already incurred to purchase the mail list.

Consider the following follow-up activities:

◻   Conduct a second mailing two weeks after the first, excluding the addresses of those who have already responded and those that were returned by the post office.

◻   Conduct a third mailing two weeks after the second.

◻   Conduct a postcard mailing.

◻   Send a follow-up e-mail.

◻   Conduct a series of follow-up telephone calls.

Direct E-Mail

An e-mail campaign has several advantages over a traditional mail campaign sent via the post office. It is less expensive because there are no stationery, printing, or postage costs. It is also more likely to reach the eyeballs of your prospects, because most people open their own e-mail. Most importantly, an e-mail approach provides a more efficient method for prospects to respond to you quickly. They can simply click on a link to your e-mail address or website.

There are, however, several challenges to conducting an e-mail campaign. First, it is often more difficult to obtain e-mail addresses than snail mail addresses. This is especially true if you plan to assemble your own database by searching the Web. To avoid excessive spam, many company websites don't provide the e-mail addresses of employees.

A second challenge with e-mail campaigns is that your e-mails may not reach their destination because they will have to traverse through one or more spam filters along the way.

A third problem is that even if your message reaches the prospect, it may be viewed as spam and deleted before it is opened. Although discarding is a problem with traditional mail as well, some recipients become outraged when they receive spam. It is possible, although not likely, that some recipients of your direct e-mail might contact your Internet Service Provider (ISP) and try to have you labeled as a spammer. You will need to decide whether or not you are willing to take this risk.

The five steps involved in conducting a direct e-mail campaign are similar to the steps involved in conducting a direct mail campaign discussed above.

Step 1: Plan the campaign. The major issues to consider ahead of time are: what type of follow-up you will conduct (e.g., multiple e-mail messages, telephone, direct mail); whether you will prepare a simple text e-mail message or a more complex html message; whether you will send out the e-mails via your own e-mail program or use an html bulk mail service; and what links you will provide in the e-mail—your website, for example.

Step 2: Assemble the list. You can assemble your e-mail list from contact information in your own database, or you can gather e-mail addresses from membership directories of professional associations or from information available on the Web. E-mail lists can also be purchased from mailing list providers.

Step 3: Write the e-mail message. It is important to keep the message short and focused on a problem that your prospects may be facing, rather than on your own qualifications. Make it about the prospect and not about you, although certainly include relevant links to your website and your contact information. It is also important that you include "opt-out" instructions so that recipients have the option of asking you to remove them from your e-mail list.

Step 4: Launch the campaign. The easiest approach is to prepare a text message and send it out using your own e-mail program through your own ISP. This approach, however, has its limitations. Many ISPs have a limit as to how many messages you can send simultaneously. For some, it is as few as fifteen or twenty. This can make sending a message to several hundred or more prospects quite time-consuming. If you use this approach, it is very important that you place your own e-mail address in the "To" section and use the bcc section for the e-mail addresses of the prospects. This way the recipients will not have to wade through a long list of the other recipients, and it also protects their privacy.

Sending a plain text e-mail message will increase your chances of bypassing spam filters. This means no bold, underlining, italics, color, or graphics. The downside is that it will look plain, even unprofessional, but it will probably reach more people.

A better alternative is to use a bulk e-mail service. These services allow you to create an html e-mail message with all types of formatting. They have standard templates that are easy to use, or you can create your own interface that includes your logo, the colors you use on your website, graphics, photos, and your signature. Once you upload your list of prospect e-mail addresses, these e-mail services can also send your message in both text and html versions. That way, if your prospect cannot receive an html version, they will automatically be sent the text version. Another option is to send a text e-mail message via your own e-mail program and ISP, but in the first paragraph of the message include a link to an html version of the letter, which you prepare ahead of time on your website.

Step 5: Follow up. E-mail campaigns can be followed up with additional e-mail messages, telephone calls, letters, or postcards.

Cold Calling

It's 6:00 P.M. You are sitting around the dinner table with your family and the phone rings. You check the caller ID and see that it is another annoying sales call trying to sell you a credit card or telephone service. You say to your family, "Nobody buys from telemarketers. Why on earth do they call?" You would be wrong. Cold calling *does* work. The reason that telemarketers keep calling is because they know the exact ratio of sales per number of calls and have concluded that it is profitable. It can be for you as well, if you have the fortitude to do it.

One day I was sitting at my desk when the phone rang. It was one of those recorded messages. You know the type—the kind that you hang up on immediately. But this time I listened for a few moments. It was from the president of a home restoration and repair company. The timing was just right for me. On my to-do list for the past three months had been to find someone to fix the water damage from an old leak in our living room. I had already received the check from the insurance company but had never gotten around to trying to find the right person to make the repair. I listened to the recording, jotted down the phone number, and immediately called this company's president. I told him about the damage and how much the insurance company said the repair should cost. He agreed to the amount, and the next day two of his subcontractors fixed the damage. It was all about timing. His ice-cold phone call came at just the right moment.

You may be thinking that you are selling professional services, not restoration services, credit cards, or telephone services, and that cold calling will not work for you. But if you call the right people, in the right way, and catch them at the right time, cold calls can definitely win you business.

Cold calling, in which you attempt to reach your prospect directly, is another direct marketing technique. Many consultants have an aversion to making cold calls because they do not feel comfortable calling strangers. This is understandable. But if conducted properly, cold calling can be very effective. Like any other marketing technique, you have to learn how to overcome the challenges. Develop a system, work the system, fine-tune it, and you will eventually become comfortable.

Here are the four basic steps of a cold calling campaign:

Step 1: Assemble the call list. Just as with a direct mail effort, the quality of your list is critical. The list should consist of those who are likely to have a need for your service or are feeling a pain that you can alleviate. It should be comprised of decision-makers (i.e., those who have the authority and budget to hire you). Calling only gatekeepers and those who can merely recommend you to others is a prescription for failure. Needless to say, direct phone numbers are much better than main office phone numbers. Ideally, you will also know the pronunciation of each prospect's name, whether the prospect is male or female, and what name they prefer to use (e.g., Rob or Bob rather than Robert).

Step 2: Develop a strategy. You need to have a plan, which should address such questions as:

▫ **What is the objective of the phone call (i.e., a meeting, an invitation to write a proposal, or to close the sale)?** For most consultants, a sale will rarely ever be made without a face-to-face meeting. In this case, a meeting is probably a good objective.

▫ **What time of day should I call (morning, lunchtime, afternoon, late afternoon, or after work hours)?** An advantage of the morning is that both you and your prospect will be more energetic. Very early morning, lunchtime, and after work hours all have the advantage that a secretary is less likely to field your call. Some cold callers like to call after hours. Instead of speaking to the prospect, they plan to leave a detailed voice message with the hope that the prospect will then visit their website or call them back if interested.

▫ **Will I leave a voice message?** Most cold callers prefer not to leave voice messages because what they really want to do is speak with the prospect. Leaving a voice message with the hope that the prospect will call back is a strategy that can work and is preferred by some cold callers, but you should know that the likelihood of a call back is very low.

▫ **If I am going to leave a voice message, how many messages will I leave?** This must be given careful consideration. Leaving many voice messages, even if separated by several weeks, can be annoying to a prospect.

❑ **What will I say in the voice message?** Prepare a script and practice it until you don't fumble your words, so that it seems natural and unscripted. Get to the point quickly, and be certain to clearly give your contact information.

❑ **What will I say if a secretary or receptionist answers?** Ask if the prospect is available. If they are not available, ask, "When would be a good time to call back?" If you are asked to give your name and phone number, by all means do so, but you also may want to say that you will try again at another time. Or ask if you can leave a voice message. Secretaries often prefer that anyway, since it relieves them of the responsibility of writing down, prioritizing, and delivering the message.

❑ **How will I follow up?** For example, you may want to plan on leaving three messages separated by a week, then sending several direct mail letters, and following up with another phone call.

❑ **Will I be the one making the phone calls?** There is an advantage to having an experienced cold caller or someone you train conduct the calls for you. It can raise the level of your credibility. To save the cost of contracting or hiring someone, consider this: Team up with a fellow consultant who provides a service that doesn't compete with yours. You agree to make cold calls for your buddy if your buddy makes them for you.

Step 3: Develop a script. Suzanne Paling of Sales Management Services (www.salesmanagementservices.com), a consultant who often trains cold callers, offers the following advice when developing a script:

❑ Begin by introducing yourself.

❑ Don't ask, "How are you?" Most prospects don't like this question.

❑ Get to the point quickly.

❑ Don't ask yes or no questions. Instead, prepare three or four open-ended questions that will encourage the prospect to talk. These questions might begin with phrases such as:

"Ever thought about …?"

"Have you been considering …?"

"Tell me a little about how you deal with the problem of …"

- Talk about the benefits your services provide rather than the specific features of your services or experience.

- Ask general, easy-to-answer questions that don't put the prospect on the spot. Questions such as "How would you like to proceed?" are better than questions like "Are you budgeted for this?" or "When does the committee meet to discuss this?"

- Never read from the script. Merely use it as a guide.

Susan Salvo of Revenue Generators (www.revenuegenerators.net) is an independent consultant who conducts cold calls for companies and other independent consultants. She suggests using qualifying questions in your script like, "Do you use outside consultants for your ___ work?" If they do, you can probe further to learn more about what they might need. If they tell you they do not, then you can ask about the conditions that might warrant them to use an outside consultant in the future.

Step 4: Make the calls. Conducting cold calls is one of the most challenging marketing tasks a consultant can undertake. It is important to develop the right mindset. The overwhelming majority of the calls you make will not be successful. That's the nature of this game. You therefore need to prepare yourself for rejection. Recognize that the only way you will make a sale is by plowing through many unsuccessful calls. Here are a few other tips:

- Warm up your voice before you make the first call. An easy way to do this is to sing the vowel sounds *ah* (as in fog), *eh* (as in bed), *i* (as in sit), *oh* (as in soap), and *oo* (as in spoon) to the tune of the musical scale Doe-Ray-Mee-Fah-So. Repeat this slowly five or six times. You might want to close the door first, but you will be amazed at how effectively this gets your vocal cords ready.

- Practice using the script each time you begin your daily calls.

- Consider standing up when you make the calls. It gives you more energy and makes you sound more alive.

- Smile while you speak. Don't ask me how, but this makes you seem warmer and more pleasant.

- Don't use a speakerphone. Although it might be more comfortable for you, the connection with your prospect will not be as clear.

◻ Be professional at all times. Never lose your temper.

◻ Set a specific goal for how many calls you will make during an hour, a morning, or a day, and make sure you meet that goal.

◻ Don't rush too quickly to accept a prospect's request of, "Why don't you send me something in the mail?" This is usually their way of just getting you off the phone. Ask them what they would like you to send, followed by when you could call them back to discuss it. Or say something direct, like "I have a lot of literature that I could send to you, but often when people ask me to send something they are really saying that they are not interested. Is that the case?"

◻ If the prospect says that they are not the right person, ask, "Who is the right person?" "What is his or her phone number?" and "Can I tell them that you suggested I call?"

◻ Keep legible and accurate records of who you called and what happened when you made the call (e.g., left a voice message, left a message with a secretary, spoke directly with the prospect and learned ...).

Conclusion

Don't rule out direct marketing for your consulting services. The three approaches discussed in this chapter (i.e., direct mail, direct e-mail, and cold calling) can be effective strategies for most consulting businesses. They enable you to make contact with people outside of your immediate circle of contacts. The challenge is to entice people who don't know or trust you to believe that you can help them.

The keys to successful direct marketing campaigns are to:

◻ Make certain that you address real needs your prospects are experiencing.

◻ Contact the appropriate people.

◻ Follow up diligently.

◻ Spend the time and energy needed to properly plan and executive the campaign.

CHAPTER 8

Marketing Your Services Through Writing

GOOGLE PROVIDES A GREAT SERVICE called "Google Alerts." It is like a newspaper clipping service for the Web. Enter a name, a phrase, or a few key words, and it will search the Web looking for a match. When it finds a match, you receive an e-mail message containing a link to the article or story that used those words. I have many of these alerts set up, including alerts for my name and the titles of the books that I have written.

One day I received a Google Alert informing me that my book was mentioned on the Web. I clicked on the link and found a review. Fortunately, it was a favorable review. It also contained the e-mail address of the person who wrote the review. I Googled his name and found that he was a senior executive at one of the largest companies in India. I e-mailed him, saying that I was delighted he liked the book and offered to help him or any of his companies if there should be a need for my services.

Several weeks later he e-mailed me back, saying that he agreed with my book's thesis that employees join organizations but leave their managers. He invited me to come to India to speak to groups of senior executives about how to reduce employee attrition.

I generally do not market internationally and had never performed any work in India. This is business I never would have landed without having written a book.

But you don't have to write a book in order to land new business. Writing articles, letters to the editor, white papers, and electronic newsletters can all lead to new business.

I received a phone call one day from the CEO of a community hospital in Wisconsin. He said that he had read an article I had written on employee pride and that he was trying to improve pride in his organization. I had written the article as part of my monthly e-newsletter. He had read it in one of the many newspapers and websites that often reproduce my articles. Sight unseen, on the strength of the article, I was hired to help his hospital improve employee pride.

Here is another example. I received a phone call one day from the executive director of a large public library in a major Southern U.S. city. She knew about my book and therefore knew that I conducted employee surveys. She wanted me to help her conduct a survey of her library staff. When I asked how she had heard about my book, she said, "I'm a librarian."

The Challenge

If you provide people with valuable information and distribute your writing regularly and to a wide audience, it will lead to new business. There are three major writing challenges all consultants face:

1. **Value:** Your writing cannot merely be an advertisement for your professional services. It has to address real needs in the marketplace. Otherwise, nobody is going to read it. Of course, you do not want to give away trade secrets or information that your clients should pay to receive. But by providing readers with information that is useful, you will show the world that you are an expert and worth hiring.

2. **Consistency:** Writing an article once a year will not do the trick,

unless of course it is a seminal article and appears in the most prestigious publication in your field. You need to write often.

3. **Distribution:** Your writing needs to be distributed to people who may hire you or to those who know people who can hire you. You do not have to publish an article every year in the *Harvard Business Review* to land new business. For example, if you consult to a small niche and produce a value-laden electronic newsletter that reaches the major players in that niche, you are probably in good shape. But if your newsletter is not reaching the appropriate people and is published infrequently, your writing will probably not lead to new business.

Solutions

This chapter describes six approaches to marketing your consulting services: writing white papers, publishing articles, publishing books, publishing a print newsletter, publishing an electronic newsletter, and writing a blog.

Write White Papers

A white paper is an authoritative report that addresses a specific issue or problem. It is a marketing technique used to educate people in your target market and to demonstrate your knowledge, thoughtfulness, and credibility.

For example, one of the groups I target is senior human resource professionals. Periodically I produce white papers that I believe will interest them. I conducted an interview study of senior human resource professionals about the skills and abilities needed to succeed as a senior human resource professional, and I prepared a report about the findings. Another time I wrote about a survey I had conducted of vice presidents of human resources concerning their views of their own jobs, their roles in their organization, and their plans for the future. Both of these reports promoted the fact that I conduct employee surveys. I e-mailed them to participants in the study and to other prospects. I also made them available for download on my website.

Writing and distributing a white paper probably will not yield immediate new clients. But if you write many of them and distribute them widely to the appropriate people, they will eventually bring you business. It is important that well-written papers address a concern of your target market and provide your contact information.

White papers can be distributed in many ways. You can include them in direct mail packages, send them along with your proposals, hand them out at meetings with prospects, and make them available for download from your website.

Here are a few key points to keep in mind when preparing white papers:

- **Pick a topic that is important to your prospects.** It should address a problem, a concern, or other issue that you know will interest them.

- **Choose a topic that can lead to new business.** Avoid writing about a problem that you can't fix. It should be obvious from the topic of the paper that you have the expertise and experience to solve the problem.

- **Avoid basing the white paper on the views of others.** If you quote others extensively in your white paper, your prospects will be more likely to contact those you have quoted than you. Let those other experts do their own marketing. If you don't have the expertise yourself to write the paper, pick another topic.

- **Stick to evergreen topics that will not become quickly dated.** That way, your white paper will have some shelf life, and you will be able to use it for several years or perhaps even longer.

- **Make certain to include your contact information.** Remember, this is a marketing piece. It should be very easy for someone to figure out how to contact you via telephone, fax, snail mail, and e-mail.

- **Pay careful attention to the title.** The title needs to grab the reader. Lists are often effective. For example, "Ten Reasons Why You Need to Plan Now for Inflation," or "Seven Reasons Why It Makes Sense for Your Company to Go Green."

- **Make it easy to read by using a legible font.** If possible, use artwork, graphics, charts, and figures to communicate your message.

- **Desktop publish and print the white paper.** This will make it look much more professional than a simple printout of text. Consider having the paper printed on a glossy stock and including your picture and company logo.

◘ **Remember, it's not about you.** The paper needs to demonstrate your expertise, but much more importantly, it needs to provide value to your prospects.

Publish Articles

Articles published in newspapers, trade publications, magazines, and journals have much more credibility than unpublished white papers. Rightly or wrongly, prospects assume that if someone thought well enough of your article to publish it, you must know what you're talking about. Even if your prospects don't read the article, just seeing the masthead of a reputable publication on a reprint with your byline will increase your credibility.

Bylined pieces are good mailer material, but they might also catch the attention of a qualified prospect on their own. Several years ago I wrote an article about readership surveys for *Folio,* a publication read by magazine publishers. Shortly after the article was published, I received a call from the editor of the Mayo Clinic's health newsletter, who was interested in how their readers felt about her publication. One thing led to another, and I had a new client.

Many consultants are reluctant to try to write articles because they are under the mistaken belief that it is difficult to persuade editors to publish them. But most trade publications are hungry for content. They pump out new issues monthly, weekly, or even daily and often rely on contributions from outsiders. You are the expert who can solve their problems and make their lives easier. In other words, they are looking for articles from people just like you.

It's not even necessary to set your sights too high. Unless you are a scholar in your field, it might be difficult for you to get an article placed in an academic or scientific journal. Top-tier publications like the *Harvard Business Review* or *BusinessWeek* might also be difficult to crack.

That said, there are thousands of publications that need content. It is important to target publications that are credible and read by your target market. If you are working in a niche market, then it is probably obvious to you what publications your prospects read. If you are uncertain, simply ask your current clients.

Here are the steps to getting an article published:

Step 1: Target the appropriate publication. Target publications that you believe will increase your credibility. For example, a few years ago I wrote an article for the *Journal of Business Strategy*. I had never heard of this publication and was fairly confident none of my clients read it. But it is a professional, credible journal, and the impressive-looking reprint helped me land several clients.

Some publications will pay you to write an article for them. This is a nice bonus, but the fee will probably be modest. Your primary purpose for writing the article is to help you gain credibility in the marketplace.

Ideally, the publication will allow you to include a paragraph at the end of the article that says something about your business and provides your contact information. Some publications have strict policies against this. You may want to steer away from them. On the other hand, you could publish the article without your contact information and then include it when you have the article reprinted.

Step 2: Contact the publication. Don't write an article before you find a home for it. Publications will often prefer a particular slant or specify the length. The article will also be stronger if you work with an editor to make certain it is directed at their target audience.

You will need to prepare a pitch, which will include a brief summary of the article. The pitch should be an idea that will meet both the needs of the publication (i.e., satisfying the interests of their readers) as well as your needs (i.e., promoting your consulting services). It can be something as simple as, "I would like to write an article for your publication about … I am confident that it will be of value to your readers because …"

Before you develop the pitch, do some homework. Take a look at a few back issues and notice how the articles from outside contributors are written. How long are they? Are they "how-to" articles, or more conceptual? How direct or subtle are they about marketing their own services? What contact information has the publisher allowed them to provide?

Some publications print their yearly editorial calendar, which lists the major topics they plan to cover in each upcoming issue. For example, their January issue may focus on financial issues, February on human resource issues, and March on marketing issues. This is valuable information that can help you target your pitch to meet the needs of the publication.

You will also need to find the name of a specific editor to contact. Often names, e-mail addresses, and phone numbers are listed in the publication. Peruse the list of editors, and target the one who seems to focus on your topic. If that information is not available, contact the managing editor. If this is not the right person, he or she will direct you to the appropriate person.

You can try to pitch an editor by telephone, but most are more likely to reply to an e-mail message than to return a phone call. Either way, editors will likely respond in one of the following ways:

- *That's great! Can you make it 750 to 1,000 words and get it to me in three weeks?*

- *That would be fine, but can you put the following slant on it?*

- *We don't need an article on that, but can you write one on … ?*

- *We may be interested, but can you first send me a sample of your writing?*

- *Can you send me an outline of the article before I make a commitment?*

- *I am sorry, but we don't think that article would be of interest to our readers.* Or, *We recently commissioned a similar article.*

If they are interested, ask when they need it, how many words they require, and whether they can accept tables, charts, or photographs.

Step 3: Write the article. The article must be well organized and easy to read. It should not be overtly promotional but should convincingly demonstrate that you are the go-to person on this topic.

The title and first paragraph should draw the reader in. One effective technique is to use a numbered list in the title. For example, "Seven Ways for Your Organization to Stay Light on Its Feet During Difficult Economic Times," or "Ten Ways to Keep Your Employees Motivated During the Slow Season." Using a title like this enables the reader to clearly understand the objective of the article and how it is organized.

Another approach is to use a title that is contrary to popular opinion or provocative in some other way. For example, when everyone is writing about the importance of saving, you might write an article titled, "Why Now is the Time to Spend." Or when everyone is writing about the importance of retaining employees, you might write an article titled, "Why Employee Turnover is Good."

The first paragraph should also draw the reader's interest. One strategy is to use an anecdotal lead in order to humanize the content of the article. For example, someone writing an article about financial planning might start with a story about a family that needed to start supporting an eighty-five-year-old mother. An article about the failing economy might begin with a brief story about an auto supply worker who has been out of work for the past six months. Take a look at any issue of the *Wall Street Journal* or the *New York Times*, and you will find plenty of examples of anecdotal leads. You can then launch into the major content of the article and perhaps conclude by referring back to the opening story in the final paragraph.

Another method for drawing the reader into the article is to begin with a statistic. Many of the articles I write begin with a statistic from the database of employee opinion survey responses that I maintain. One of the articles on leadership, for example, began with, "One out of two employees say management makes poor decisions." Another on employee retention began, "One-third of employees intend to leave their jobs in the near future."

The structure of the article must be clear to both you and the reader. Each paragraph must lead to the next. Prepare an outline of the article and stick to it. I often use the following four-part structure:

1. Open with an anecdotal lead.
2. Describe a problem faced by your prospects.
3. Follow up with several paragraphs that provide solutions to the problem.
4. Provide a conclusion that summarizes the solutions and perhaps ties them back to the initial opening anecdote.

Step 4: Leverage the article. What you do after the article is published is key. Remember, the goal is not just to publish an article; it is to land new business by establishing your credibility among potential prospects. Here is how to leverage the article.

Make reprints of the article. Some publishers insist that you order the reprints through them, since they own the copyright. (This provides them with another source of revenue.) But often you can just take a hard copy of the article to a printer, who will desktop publish and print it for you. You tell them what you want it to look like (e.g., black and white or color; one page or multiple pages; two column or three column; plain, coated, or glossy stock, etc.). If the article doesn't provide your contact information or only provides limited information, you can instruct the printer to insert additional information. One trick I learned many years ago is to have the printer leave out the publication date. This increases the shelf life of the reprint.

Once you have the reprint in hand, mail it to people in your network and to your prospects. You should also keep a supply on hand so that you can include it with your proposals or when prospects or the press ask you to send them information.

If the article you write is Web-based rather than print, e-mail the link to your network and prospects. You can also include the link on your website. Ask the editor if and when the link will expire to avoid at some point directing people to a link that leads to nowhere or to a totally different article.

Publish Books

A book, a powerful demonstration of your knowledge and competence, is the ultimate marketing piece. The effort and time commitment required to write a book is substantial, but the rewards can be worthwhile.

The two basic approaches to publishing a book are to self-publish or to publish through an established publishing company. Place a self-published book side by side with a published book, and most people will not be able to tell the difference. Each approach has its advantages and disadvantages.

If you self-publish, in addition to writing the book, you also handle the desktop publishing, designing, printing, pricing, distribution, and all the marketing. If you work through a publisher, the editing, desktop publishing, designing, printing, pricing, distribution, and some of the marketing are taken care of for you.

The advantage of self-publishing is that you have total control of the content, pricing, and all aspects related to the physical production of the book. You can publish the book according to your own schedule, and you retain the rights to reproduce, translate, and turn the book into a CD, Podcast, or movie.

Since you don't need to share the revenues from book sales with a publisher, you can also earn a greater profit from each book sold. For example, a colleague of mine who consults to the travel industry self-published a training manual for travel tour operators. He put it on two CDs, which he sells for $599. Finding a publisher to take on that type of project with such a high price tag and limited potential readership would be difficult. Another colleague self-published a book for his target market of healthcare administrators, another limited market that would probably not interest most conventional book publishers.

The primary advantages of using an established publisher include the credibility you will receive in the marketplace, their established distribution system, and their help in marketing the book to bookstores and the media. You also will not have to worry about the editing and physical production of the book. Although you will always want to participate in marketing, most publishers will conduct mailings and send sample copies to reviewers, send out press releases, and line up radio and television interviewers.

Having a published book can raise your consulting practice to another level. For example, I bring copies of my first book, *30 Reasons Employees Hate Their Managers*, to my sales meetings. At the beginning of the meeting, I give copies of the book to the prospects. It is obvious during these meetings that the book has impressed them. More importantly, handing out the book has led to more sales.

Among the disadvantages of using a publisher are that you have less control of the release date, and even of the content. Most importantly, the majority of the money from book sales goes to the publisher, not to you. For a book that retails for $21.95, don't be surprised if you end up receiving less than $2.00 per book. Although an unknown first-time author can expect to receive an advance of between $5,000 and $10,000, you will need to sell between 2,500 and 5,000 copies in order to receive any additional royalties.

Here are a few tips for finding a publisher.

- **Prepare a book proposal.** The book proposal needs to include the following elements: a one- or two-page summary of the purpose of the book (i.e., the intended audience and what information it will convey), a table of contents, a description of how the book differs from other books on the topic, a plan for how you will market the book, information about you, and up to three sample chapters.

- **Target the right publishers.** There are hundreds of publishers, specializing in everything from fiction to cookbooks to coffee-table books. Even among publishers of business books, some focus on highly technical topics, while others are interested only in books aimed at the general public. Find a publisher whose audience is the same as the audience you are targeting. When I sent the proposal for my first book to AMACOM, the editor told me she was interested, but she was not satisfied with two of the sample chapters I included. I asked her, "If you don't like the sample chapters, why are you still interested in publishing the book?" She replied, "It's exactly the type of book that we publish. It is a perfect fit for our target audience."

- **Find a book agent.** Finding a book agent can be as difficult as finding a publisher, but agents can be extremely valuable. Although they will take 10 to 15 percent of your royalties, they know the market and probably have personal relationships with the top editors who might be interested in publishing your book.

- **Find a publisher.** There are reference books in any good library that list publishers and their contact information. Another approach is to visit your local bookstore, scan the bookshelves, and take note of who publishes the books that are similar to the book you are planning to write. But by far the best method is to talk to fellow consultants who have published a book. Ask them if they will introduce you to their editors.

Whether you use a publisher or self-publish, the responsibility for marketing the book is primarily yours. Here are some effective strategies for marketing books:

- Send copies of the book to reviewers at newspapers and trade publications.

- Distribute press releases to the media (i.e., newspapers, trade publications, radio stations, and television stations) with the hope of landing interviews.

- Deliver speeches on the content of the book at trade association meetings.

- Promote the book on your website and in your print or electronic newsletter.

- Contact organizations to interest them in buying copies of the book for their employees or customers.

- Create a separate website about your book that includes the table of contents, a sample chapter, and favorable reviews.

- Invite friends and colleagues to write reviews of the book on sites such as Amazon.com.

- Advertise the book in newspapers and trade publications.

Publish a Print Newsletter

A free printed newsletter is a great way to keep in periodic contact with your network and prospects. The objective of the newsletter is to educate your readers in a way that makes you the top-of-mind go-to person when a problem or issue arises in your area of expertise.

Printed newsletters come in many forms, from a one-page typed letter, to four-color, four-page desktop-published documents printed on coated stock. The choice of format is dictated by the image you want to create and the time and money you are able to devote to its production.

No matter what format you use, there are a few general principles to keep in mind:

- **Provide value.** The newsletter can't be merely an advertisement for your services. It isn't a brochure. It should provide useful content to your readers.

- **Establish a consistent look and feel.** Just like the magazines to which you subscribe, each issue of your newsletter should have the same format, colors, type of content, and writing style. That way your readers will become accustomed to reading it and will remember it.

- **Write it yourself.** Some consultants send newsletters containing columns or entire issues written by others. This defeats your purpose. It must demonstrate your competence and knowledge, not the abilities of your colleagues.

- **Keep in mind the purpose of the newsletter.** Make certain the connection is clear between what you are writing about and the services that you offer. For example, it doesn't make any sense to write about international affairs, global warming, or the economy if your expertise is in computer networking.

- **Provide an opt-out option.** Provide a method for your readers to let you know if they no longer wish to receive your newsletter.

- **Publish it regularly.** Keeping your name and skills top-of-mind for your readers requires that you publish quarterly, monthly, or perhaps even more frequently.

A printed newsletter has a number of advantages over other forms of marketing:

- **You will stand out.** With the proliferation of electronic newsletters, printed newsletters are less common these days. This increases the probability that your words will be read and remembered.

- **It will fuel your network.** Seventy-two percent of The Consulting 200 said that the majority of their business comes from word-of-mouth referrals. This is why you must keep in close contact with your network of friends, colleagues, current clients, and former clients. They are your best source of new business. A newsletter (either printed or electronic) is an excellent method of keeping in periodic contact with your network.

- **It will keep you fresh.** Forcing yourself to publish a newsletter helps you to constantly focus and fine-tune your ideas. The more you write, the more focused you will be.

- **You will be able to leverage the content.** By continually writing, you will produce readily available content that you can use in your consulting work and speeches, in audio and video products that you might sell, and perhaps even a book you may write.

Producing a printed newsletter, however, poses a number of challenges:

◘ **A printed version of a newsletter requires a great deal of effort.** If it is two to four pages, you will need to write several articles, and that will be time-consuming. I have known many a consultant who ran out of gas and ceased publishing after their third or fourth issue.

◘ **The production of a printed newsletter is extremely intensive.** It includes writing the articles, desktop publishing, printing, folding, managing a mail address database, printing mail labels, purchasing envelopes, affixing mail labels and postage to the envelopes, and stuffing the newsletter into the envelopes. Many of these steps, however, can be outsourced or delegated to others.

◘ **The process can be expensive.** The out-of-pocket fixed costs for desktop publishing and for printing, labels, envelopes, and postage will vary, of course, depending on the number of copies you print and the number of recipients.

There are a number of ways to reduce the amount of effort and expense required to produce a printed newsletter. For example, Ruth Winett (www.winettassociates.com) keeps it simple. She produces a one-page typed newsletter on her stationery. John Haas (www.managementstrategiesgroup.com) for many years combined forces with four other consultants to produce a four-page quarterly newsletter. They invited a guest author for each issue to expand exposure. They each wrote separate articles, shared the production costs, and mailed it to their combined network.

Publish an Electronic Newsletter

An electronic newsletter is simply a newsletter sent by e-mail, and can be a powerful and highly effective marketing tool. It provides the positive value of a print newsletter (i.e., keeping you in close contact with your network by providing useful information) and offers many advantages over a print newsletter:

◘ **It costs far less.** With an electronic newsletter, there are no costs for desktop publishing, printing, stationery, or postage. You will incur only modest costs if you use an html e-mail service such as Topica or Constant Contact to house your database of readers.

◘ **It makes it much easier for readers to contact you.** Readers can simply click on a link and send you an e-mail message.

- **There is less writing involved.** Electronic newsletters, like e-mail messages, should be short. This forces you to be to the point and calls for less writing than a print newsletter requires.

- **It can be distributed more quickly.** An electronic newsletter can be written and distributed to your readers in less than a day. Good luck trying to do that with a print newsletter.

- **An electronic newsletter can include links to pages on your website.** The links could be audio or video content, access to downloadable articles, or previous newsletters you have written.

- **Readers can easily forward your newsletter to others.** In the magazine business, they call it "pass-along readership." Somewhere in each issue, you should suggest that your readers forward your newsletter to others.

- **You can determine for certain if your newsletter was delivered and opened.** With a print newsletter, you have no way of knowing whether it was actually read by your target audience. You will not know if you are using a bad address unless you send the newsletter first class and the postal service sends it back to you with the correct address. Many of the html e-mail services allow you to track which e-mail addresses were deliverable, who opened the message, and even who clicked on which of the links you provided in the newsletter.

Here are seven steps for creating an electronic newsletter and using it on an ongoing basis to market your services:

Step 1: Develop a content template. Each issue of your electronic newsletter should maintain the same style and format, and most importantly, the same structure. Having a consistent structure will make it easier for your readers to read and easier for you to write. As an example of a content template, my monthly electronic newsletter, archived at www.discoverysurveys.com/itwarchives.html, follows a six-part template. Each monthly issue dating back to January of 2000 uses the same basic formula:

- A provocative title that draws the reader into the article. Here are some of the titles I have used:

   Are You a Workaholic?

> How to Get Your Enemies at Work to Respect You
>
> The "I-Want-To-Go-Out-On-My-Own" Blues
>
> Five Sure-Fire Ways to Alienate Your Boss

- A statistic from my employee survey research. Readers enjoy statistics, and using them demonstrates the breadth of the work I have conducted over the years, and the value I can bring to my clients. Here are some statistics I have used:

  > Four out of every ten employees are dissatisfied with their work/life balance.
  >
  > One out of three employees is planning to leave for another job.
  >
  > Half of all employees say management makes poor decisions.

- An anecdote about a client, colleague, or friend that illustrates a particular real-world challenge. For instance, in an issue about workaholics, I wrote this introductory paragraph:

Nancy Halas is a senior partner in a four-doctor suburban specialty practice. She works long hours and provides excellent service to her patients. She is known as one of the best doctors in her state. But she's driving herself crazy. She's a perfectionist. She wants everything done perfectly, her way, and resents her partners and the office staff when anything is not up to her high standards. Therefore, she ends up doing most of the work herself. She resents others for "making her" do all of the work herself so that it's done just right. She's exhausted and looks forward to the day when she can retire.

In an issue about how difficult it is for organizations to accurately predict the future, I started the newsletter with this anecdote:

A letter came in the mail at my home one day last month. It was a plain white #10-sized envelope addressed to my son, Ben, with a printed return address label containing the name Ms. Ann Marie Johnson of Scarsdale, New York. My son graduated college more than a year ago and now lives in Washington, DC. I e-mailed him and asked whether he wanted me to open it or just send it to him.

The letter sat on our kitchen table for several days while my wife and I awaited his reply. We were very curious. The more we stared at the letter, the more perplexed we became. Each day my wife asked whether our son had replied to my e-mail message. He hadn't. We were tempted to open the letter even without his permission.

Then my wife realized something. She pointed to the address on the envelope and said, "I'm pretty sure that's Ben's handwriting." She also noticed that on the back, in the same handwriting, it said, "I bet it will cost 65 cents to mail this." Now we were really intrigued.

Thank goodness our son called the next day. The first thing we asked was, who is Ann Marie Johnson and did he know anything about the letter? He did not. We then told him we thought it was addressed in his handwriting. He was as puzzled as we were. He told us to go ahead and open it. Here's what we found.

We discovered that this was an exercise from his European History teacher when he was a senior in high school, five years earlier. She had asked everyone to write down their predictions for five years in the future about where they would be, what they would be doing, and the state of affairs in Europe. She then had them address the envelope. As promised, she held on to the letters for five years and mailed them.

Ben's forecasts were not completely accurate. Although he had predicted correctly that he would be living in Washington, DC, he wrote that he would be attending graduate school, which he is not. His predictions about the European Union were only partially accurate.

- The problem faced by organizations (the target market for most of my work is organizations, rather than individuals).
- Solutions, usually a bulleted list.

◻ A conclusion, often tying the solution back to the anecdote.

The newsletter also includes links to my website, several links to my e-mail address, announcements of my upcoming speeches, a link to the store on my website, and all of my contact information. Each monthly issue dating back to January of 2000 uses this same basic formula.

Several years ago, I produced another electronic newsletter, targeted to independent consultants who might need coaching to help them with their business. It had the following four-part structure:

1. A title that used the number seven. For example, some of the titles I used were: "Seven Ways to Stay Motivated as an Independent Consultant," "Seven Things Consultants Should Know About Sales," and "Seven Traps That Drive Consultants Crazy."
2. The problem consultants typically face.
3. Seven "solutions."
4. Conclusion, summarizing my recommendations.

Step 2: Brainstorm a list of topic ideas. Many consultants are intimidated by the idea of having to come up with a new topic each month. You can allay your fears somewhat by brainstorming a list of topics with your colleagues and clients, or even with family members. But remain flexible. Feel free to skip to the next topic on your list if another, more current topic occurs to you.

Step 3: Develop a design template. This is what your newsletter will look like. Will it be a plain text or html newsletter with colors and graphics, such as your logo? If you elect to use an html version, a Web designer can help you develop the template. My designer created a design template for my newsletter that matches the style and colors of my website. Many html e-mailing services provide several standard templates you can use or modify.

Step 4: Decide on logistical issues. The major decisions you will need to make are how frequently you will publish the newsletter and how you will distribute it. If you have only a small number of readers (e.g., less than 100), then you might elect to just e-mail it yourself through your Internet access provider. However, some of these providers only allow their customers to send a small number of e-mails at a time (e.g., twenty or less).

If you have a large number of subscribers on your list (several hundred or more), consider using an html e-mailing service. For a relatively modest fee, these services allow you to upload your e-mail list, format your message, send the e-mails all at once, and then keep track of such things as bounce backs, who opens the message, and who clicks on which of the links that you have included in the e-mail message.

Step 5: Create your distribution list. Send your newsletter to everyone in your network. That includes prospects, clients, colleagues, friends, and even family. You never know where your next lead will come from. Just grab their names from your address book. If you don't have e-mail addresses for everyone on the list, get them.

There are two basic strategies for adding names to your e-mail list: opt-in and opt-out. The *opt-in method* is when you send your first newsletter to everyone on your list and then ask them to let you know if they would like to continue to receive it. You also let them know that even if they sign up, they can unsubscribe at any time. The advantage of this method is that it shows that you are not a spammer and that you respect the sanctity of their mailbox.

The *opt-out method* is when you send the initial newsletter to everyone on your list and tell them that they will be receiving future issues but can unsubscribe now or anytime in the future.

I prefer the opt-out method, mainly because you will end up with more subscribers. Results vary, but generally with the opt-in method, only about 20 percent will subscribe. So if you start with a list of 200, you will be left with only 40. With the opt-out method, approximately 20 percent will opt out, so if you send your newsletter to 200 people, you'll be left with 160 subscribers. Which would you prefer, 40 or 160?

I can understand that some of you may not be comfortable with the opt-out method. But the folks on the list are not strangers to you. They are part of your network. Anyone who is upset that they are receiving your newsletter can always unsubscribe.

Step 6: Establish a process. Develop a systematic process for how you are going to put out the newsletter and a timetable that lists each step. For example, when are you going to start writing, complete the writing, and distribute the completed newsletter? It is important that you make the process as painless as possible and that you stick to your schedule. My process involves the following five steps:

1. First I write a draft.
2. My editor, co-writer Adam Snyder, reviews it. (It is good to have another set of eyes.)
3. I submit the edited copy to my Webmaster.
4. My Webmaster converts the newsletter to my design template and loads it onto the html e-mail program. He also creates a print-only version on my website and archives the previous issue.
5. I push a button and the message is sent to my 3,000-plus sub-scribers.

Step 7: Conduct ongoing maintenance activities. Gather feedback from subscribers about the content and any changes that they sug-gest. Keep track of how many people open the newsletter, which links are clicked, and how many people subscribe and unsubscribe.

You should also maintain and adjust your database of e-mail addresses. If e-mails are bouncing back to you, you may have the wrong e-mail address, or you may need to ask these individuals to put you on their white list so that they receive your newsletters. (A white list is a list of e-mail addresses that you mark in advance so that your e-mail program will allow them to reach you, not treat them as spam.)

Keep track of how the newsletter impacts your business. Monitor the number of prospects who contact you, invitations you receive to speak, and clients you land as a result of your newsletter.

Keep in mind, however, that the impact of your newsletter may be difficult to measure. For example, if a former client contacts you, unless she specifically mentions she has just read your newsletter, you won't know if that's why she remembered you. But that may very well be the reason why you were top-of-mind.

Write a Blog

By helping keep you in contact with your network, a blog can serve many of the same functions as an electronic newsletter. Basically, a blog is a website that provides regular short entries of commentary and opinions, usually presented in reverse-chronological order. Blogs by consultants can be housed on their website or on a separate site. They typically include text, images, and links to the consultant's Web pages and websites. If you can create a loyal following of visitors who frequent your blog, you will be able to create a buzz that may indeed lead to new business.

There are a few differences between a blog and an electronic newsletter. First, a blog invites readers to comment on the author's entries. These comments are visible to both the author and everyone else who visits the blog. In active blogs, there is a running commentary between the author and the readers and among readers and other readers.

Second, most blogs are passive portals. Visitors must intentionally visit them to determine whether you have a new post and to enter into dialog. This differs from an electronic newsletter that you deliver to your subscribers. Of course, it is possible to e-mail your network a message about your latest blog entry and encourage readers to click on a link that will take them there.

Third, a blog is open to everyone. Anyone on the World Wide Web can visit it. They just need to know that your blog exists and find the URL. This is different from a newsletter, which is only received by the network you send it to.

Conclusion

Writing is a critically important part of any marketing effort. Whether you are writing a book, article, white paper, newsletter, or blog, there are a few basic principles that should guide your approach.

- **Provide value.** Your writing should not only promote your services. In order to be effective, it needs to be useful to others. It must provide a perspective, a point of view, or actionable items that help solve problems. If you can do this on a consistent basis, prospects will eventually seek your help.
- **Use a formula.** Develop a design template, a structure, or an approach that you can use on a consistent basis. This will make it easier for you to write and easier for your audience to read.

- **Leverage your content.** Do not reinvent the wheel each time you write. For example, reuse content that you develop for a newsletter in white papers, articles, and a book. Present the ideas in different ways each time, or use different examples.

- **Get help.** Ask for, barter, or pay someone to help you edit your writing. Find someone who cannot only correct your grammar and punctuation, but who will also say things like, "That's obvious," "Provide another example," "You should also mention this," and "You need to clarify that point."

- **Write consistently.** Put yourself on a schedule to force yourself to write on a consistent basis. Writing an article only when the fancy strikes you will not help you nearly as much as writing on a weekly or monthly basis, or even more frequently.

CHAPTER 9

Marketing Your Consulting Through Speaking

S PEAKING IS ANOTHER EXCELLENT METHOD of marketing professional services. Fifty-eight percent of The Consulting 200 reported that they deliver speeches on a consistent basis, and one-third say that it is one of their most effective marketing strategies.

Lisa Dennis (www.knowledgence.com) is a Boston-based marketing and sales consultant who has had success landing new business by delivering speeches. She works with another consultant who specializes in finding speaking opportunities for consultants. She says that she typically receives one to three good leads from each speech.

A few years ago, she had an opportunity to speak at an all-day event in Omaha, Nebraska, sponsored by the American Marketing Association. Her talk was titled "How to Create Customer-Focused Value Propositions." The audience consisted of approximately 100 marketing professionals from local businesses.

As usual, at the end of the speech Lisa offered to e-mail the highlights of her talk to those who gave her their business cards. Five months later she received an e-mail from the first vice president of group marketing communications at Mutual of Omaha. This person and five of her direct reports had attended the talk and had been using the information Lisa had provided. The vice president invited Lisa to come to Nebraska to train others in the group. Since then Lisa has delivered the training numerous times to other parts of the company.

Several years ago I had the opportunity to speak to a small networking group of senior human resource professionals in New England. They get together on a monthly basis to discuss job search strategies and to support one another. Since many of them were consulting or seeking consulting work to tide them over during their job searches, they invited me to speak about starting a consulting business.

This was an ideal opportunity for me. I knew that most of them would eventually land a corporate human resource job and perhaps remember me when they needed the type of consulting services that I offer.

That's exactly what happened. One of the people who attended the meeting worked as an HR consultant for a growing firm in my area. He persuaded his client to hire me to conduct employee focus groups. They eventually hired him full time, and he has hired me several times to conduct other types of consulting work.

The Challenge

There are three challenges to marketing your services through speaking: landing speaking opportunities, delivering a great speech, and converting members of the audience into clients:

1. **Landing speaking opportunities.** You need to speak at the right venues on the right topic. Ideally, you will speak to your target market, or to those who can easily lead you to your target market, on a topic that is directly relevant to the consulting services you provide.

2. **Delivering a great speech.** Needless to say, your talk must leave a favorable impression on the audience. Not only do you need to provide valuable information, you need to entertain, engage, and inspire.

3. **Converting members of the audience into clients.** You can deliv-

er a great speech to the right audience, but if it doesn't lead to new business, then you have wasted valuable time and energy.

Solutions

This chapter discusses two approaches to marketing through the spoken word: delivering speeches and teaching courses. Ideally, you will be paid for a speech. However, often it is worthwhile to deliver a speech to the right audience for free. For most consultants, fees from new business will be much more lucrative than a speaking fee.

Deliver Speeches

Here are the six basic steps for landing speaking opportunities and using them to market your services:

Step 1: Plan your marketing. It is important that you speak to the right people. If your target market is vice presidents of information technology, it doesn't make sense for you to speak at your local Rotary Club or to a meeting of human resource professionals. Ideally, you will speak to people who can hire you, or at least to people who can recommend you to others.

It is also important that you speak on the right topic. It needs to be something that addresses a problem faced by your target market and demonstrates your expertise. You don't want to "give away the store" or provide free consulting services during your speech. Instead you want to provide just enough value that the audience will be clamoring for more and, ideally, want to hire you to help them and their organization.

Step 2: Book the speaking engagement. Landing free speaking engagements is not as challenging as it may seem. First you need to identify appropriate professional associations, community organizations, or professional networking groups. Ideally, it will be a group whose meetings you already attend. Or ask your clients and colleagues what professional meetings and conferences they attend. Also ask them if they know any of the officers of the group or any members of the program committee.

If you can't find this information through your network, scan the Web. Often the websites of professional associations contain contact information, a schedule of upcoming events, information about past speakers, and the names and contact information of the group's officers and program chair. You can also learn from the websites how often they meet, the dates of upcoming events, the type of speakers they have used in the past, the topics that have been presented, the group's sophistication, and the problems their members are facing.

Telephone, e-mail, or write the appropriate people in the association and tell them about your desire to speak to the group at one of their upcoming meetings. Be sure to tell them how what you have to say will be of value to the group and that you are willing to speak for no charge. Then tell them that you would like to speak with them to learn more about their membership and how your presentation can be useful. Send along information about yourself, a link to your website, testimonials about your speaking, and perhaps a relevant paper you have written.

Step 3: Prepare the speech. Once you have scheduled the speaking engagement, make certain your message meets the needs of the group. Using a canned speech you have delivered many times won't be nearly as effective as a speech customized to your audience. Arrange to interview the officers of the association and several key members and probe for what information or emphasis the members will find useful.

During your interviews it is also important to find out the style of presentation the group prefers. For example, some groups like lectures, while others want the group involved in some type of interaction.

Prepare an introduction that speaks about you, your clients, and your relevant expertise. Identify who will introduce you and send that person the introduction in advance. (Bring an extra copy to the talk in case they lose it.)

In addition, prepare some type of handout that covers the key points of the presentation. Make certain it includes your contact information.

If you are using a PowerPoint presentation, some groups prefer that you distribute a copy of your slides so that the audience can use it to take notes. My speaking coach, Tom Kennedy (www.kennedy-groupboston.com), discourages the use of PowerPoint unless you plan to use it as a visual aid. Reading bullet points from your slides is distracting and tends to bore audiences, so I typically no longer use them. In fact, audiences often applaud when I announce at the start of my talks that I won't be using a PowerPoint presentation.

Step 4: Conduct the speech. Here are a couple of pointers about delivering effective, compelling speeches.

◻ **Warm up your voice before you speak.** You don't want to lose your voice during a speech. Also, keep a glass of water nearby.

◻ **Develop the appropriate mindset prior to the speech.** The great Russian theater director Constantin Stanislavski, in his classic book, *An Actor Prepares*[3] wrote about the importance of developing mental focus when you deliver your lines. This, he explained, is because communicating with your audience is, in large part, an unconscious process. If your mind is in the right place, your audience will better understand your words. For this reason, it is helpful to have what I call a "point of concentration" when you begin your speech. This is something that you focus on that will help you to better communicate with your audience. It could be something as simple as, "I really want to help these people solve their problem with ..." or "I really empathize with the difficulty these people are having."

◻ **The opening and closing are the most important parts of a good speech.** To open a speech, begin with a story, a statistic, or an anecdote. No need to bore the audience with "Thank you very much for inviting me today." The close should be something inspirational, like a story related to the theme of the speech. Don't just conclude with "Thank you, are there any questions?" I often stop just before the end and say, "Before I close this pre-sentation, are there any questions?" That way, you can end on a high note with your great closing.

◻ **Follow an effective speech template.** One effective speech template is to tell your audience at the outset what you are going to be speaking to them about, then tell them, and conclude by summarizing what you have just spoken about.

---

[3] Stanislavski, C., *An Actor Prepares*. Theater Acts, Inc. New York, 1964.

◻ **Rehearse your speech several times so that you feel comfortable with it and have a good feel for the timing.** It is also a good idea to practice in front of others so you can receive some critical feedback. Test out your stories and jokes on colleagues, friends, and family members.

During a speech I delivered in India to an English-speaking audience, I learned the hard way that even your best jokes may not always work with every audience. My opening joke in front of 160 senior executives went over like a lead balloon. You can listen to that story on my home page at www.DiscoverySurveys.com.

My second joke to this audience also bombed. I told the group to turn to the last page of their workbook, where they found a picture of a cell phone covered by a red circle and a big red X. I told them if they hear someone's cell phone ringing during the workshop, they should quickly turn to this page, rip it out of the binder, crumple it up, and throw it at the offending person. They looked at me like I was from outer space. This joke clearly did not transfer well from one culture to another. The workshop went well, but the rough beginning could have been avoided if I had run the jokes by my client ahead of time.

◻ **Customize your speech for your audience so that you can use the appropriate jargon and examples.** This will also help you to understand topics that are sensitive or inappropriate. For instance, I was delivering an outplacement workshop for employees who had just been laid off from a nonprofit organization devoted to finding new homes for pets. At one point, I started writing a list of other employment settings where they could be working with animals on a flip chart. To my surprise, when I wrote pet stores and zoos on the list, they were terribly offended.

◻ **Include plenty of anecdotes.** In fact, the speeches of many of the best speakers consist entirely of stories. Stories are like audio pictures; they each convey more than a thousand words can, and audiences love them. Find or create stories that make your major points and then practice telling them. A story can be an example of when you used a particular technique with a client or about a problem that the members of your audience are probably experiencing. Next time you listen to a good speaker, see if you can identify and count the number of stories. But don't steal them; make up your own.

◘ **Maintain eye contact with your audience.** One of the most important techniques a good speaker should use is actually the opposite of speaking—it's listening. Oral communication is a two-way process. Observe when your audience is interested, confused, engaged, or bored. Then make the appropriate adjustments.

◘ **Encourage questions and participation.** The more interaction you can have with an audience the better. Ask questions, and encourage the audience to ask questions of you. Don't wait until the end of your presentation, and make certain you stay focused on your major points and that you keep to your allotted time. Be sure to repeat questions posed by the audience, because you are probably the only person in the room with a microphone.

◘ **Remember you are an entertainer.** All speakers should realize that although their job is to inform and educate, they have the responsibility to entertain the audience as well. Use stories, humor, and anything else to make certain the audience members enjoy themselves. If they do, they are more likely to remember you, contact you when they have another need for your service, and recommend you to others.

◘ **Never read from a script.** You can use notes, but look at them only periodically. The notes should contain a major outline of your talk or list the key stories you are going to tell.

◘ **Do not take the evaluation forms too seriously.** You will never please everyone. Some will provide you with negative ratings because they are having a bad day, because they think they know more about the topic than you do, or because they enjoy being critical. The true proof of the success of your speech is whether your audience uses the information and whether they leave with an inclination to hire you again someday.

◘ **Do not overtly promote your services.** Spending too much time on self-promotion while you are on stage will turn off your audience and make them view you unfavorably. By all means, subtly promote yourself by demonstrating your competence, showing a sincere desire to help, and showcasing your experience by providing examples of how you have helped others. Be careful, however, not to be boastful.

Step 5: Maximize the marketing value of the speech. Make certain that your handout includes your contact information. Also, try to collect as many business cards and e-mail addresses as possible. Here are a few ways to do this:

▢ **Hold a drawing.** Bring an attractive bag or bowl and tell the audience that if they would like to participate in a drawing for a copy of your book (or something else of value), they can place their card in the bowl that you will pass around.

▢ **Circulate a clipboard.** I often ask the person who is introducing me to tell the audience that if they would like to receive a copy of Dr. Katcher's free electronic newsletter, simply write their name and e-mail address on the sign-up sheet that will be passed around.

▢ **Use your own evaluation sheets.** Ask the meeting planner to distribute sheets that you have prepared that ask people to provide comments on your talk. It should also invite them to provide their contact information if they would like to receive a summary of the speech, sign up for your newsletter, suggest another group that might be interested in the presentation, or speak to you about a problem their organization is facing.

Step 6: Follow up. It is important that you follow up as soon as possible with anyone who gave you their card or provided their contact information. You want to contact them while your words and the favorable impression you left are still fresh in their minds.

Teach a Course

Another way of reaching out to the community to market your services is to teach a course. I know several independent consultants who are adjunct professors one or two nights a week at a local college. I also know of several independent consultants who market their services by teaching in adult continuing education courses. One is a financial adviser, another a nutritionist, and a third is a home computer consultant.

Here are some words of advice if you are going to use this approach:

▢ **Recognize that compensation for this sort of teaching will be modest.** Adjunct professors are not paid nearly as well as fulltime professors. You will be fortunate to earn $5,000 for a fourteen-session class. If you teach a community adult education class, you might earn only $50 or less per night.

◻ **Teach in your specialty area.** If you are hoping to land business through your teaching, you should be teaching in the areas in which you consult.

◻ **Target your prospects.** Make certain that any class you teach has students who are likely prospects for your services. For example, continuing education or evening graduate classes are more likely than traditional undergraduate schools to be attended by adults employed fulltime who might be prospects for your services.

◻ **Be subtle.** Most colleges and continuing education programs frown on instructors trying to market their services to students. You will probably want to wait until the semester is over before formally approaching them about possible work.

Conclusion

Speaking can be a powerful method of marketing your consulting services. Here are some important tips:

◻ **Be strategic about where you speak.** It is important to speak to the right groups on topics that will enable you to impart value, impress, and gain new clients.

◻ **Improve your speaking skills.** No matter how many speeches you have given and how much praise you have received about your speaking abilities, there is always room for improvement. You might even want to engage the services of a speaking coach to help you fine-tune your message and improve your delivery.

◻ **Practice your speeches several times before each presentation.** This holds true even if it is a speech you have given many times.

◻ **Remember your objective.** Your goal is to convert members of the audience into clients. Make it as easy as possible for audience members to contact you.

CHAPTER 10

Maintaining Your Visibility

MARGIE DANA (www.printbuyersinternational.com) turned her consulting business into a professional association made up of printers, companies that buy printing services, designers, and companies that sell products and services to printers. In order to maintain her visibility among these constituents:

- She changes her website on a weekly basis, which places her higher on search engines and entices members to visit the site frequently.

- She publishes a weekly electronic newsletter, which contains links to her website. Back issues are also archived on the site.

- She sends direct e-mail to people who have asked to be sent information about upcoming events.

- She includes links on her site to websites of interest to her constituents. This increases traffic to her website.

- She arranges for other sites to include links to her website.

- She writes articles for other websites and electronic newsletters.

▫ She places advertisements on other websites and electronic newsletters.

▫ She manages a discussion group on the social networking site LinkedIn that includes links to her website.

▫ She writes press releases for the national media about upcoming events sponsored by her association.

▫ She speaks frequently to industry groups.

The Challenge

The people to whom you need to market your services inhabit three overlapping circles. The small innermost circle consists of people who already know and respect you. Most of your marketing should focus on these people because they are the most likely to do business with you or refer you to others. Networking and including them on your newsletter distribution list are the best ways to market to these people.

The larger middle circle consists of people you can readily identify as likely prospects. These include people who work in companies likely to need your services, who work in your geographical area, who work in the type of companies you usually serve, or who possess job titles that match your typical client profile. You probably know what publications they read and what professional meetings they attend. You could assemble or purchase a list containing their contact information. You can reach them through direct marketing, speaking, and writing.

The first two circles represent the tip of the iceberg. There is also a very large outer ring of people who also deserve your attention. They are not as easily identifiable, however. People in this ring might include those outside of your geographic area, people with job titles that don't match your typical client profile, and those who cannot use your services but could recommend you to others. This outer ring of people is more difficult to reach.

Solutions

Maintaining visibility among your outer ring requires broad marketing strategies, such as maintaining a good website, advertising, writing press releases, and conducting radio and television interviews.

Maintain a Website

It is important for independent consultants to maintain a website. A website serves as your brochure. It defines who you are and what you do and helps to establish your credibility in the marketplace. Without a website, you could be viewed as just someone in between jobs, rather than a legitimate consultant. A website will also make you reachable beyond your network. If you include the proper key words on your site, your prospects will be able to find you by conducting Web searches.

Launching an attractive, effective website will take a lot of thought about what you want the site to look like, what image you want to convey, and what information you want to include. Here are four steps to getting the process started:

Step 1: Establish your area of cyberspace. When you create a website, you will contract with an Internet Access Provider to rent space on their computer server. Companies that provide this service typically charge monthly, and the fees vary widely. You may want to consider using the provider you currently use for Web access, but in today's environment, there are companies that offer extremely low rates in return for your business.

Step 2: Reserve your domain name. Search on the Web with the phrase "reserve a domain name," and you will find many companies that provide domain name registration services. They will allow you, at no charge, to search your company's name or any other name or phrase you are interested in as a domain name in order to determine if it is available. If it is unavailable, most sites suggest similar names that *are* available. Once you settle on a domain name that hasn't been taken, you will be able to establish it as your own for a relatively modest annual fee.

Step 3: Conceptualize your site. Websites come in many forms, but it is important that your site looks professional and conveys the appropriate image. Scan the Web and take a look at the sites of your competitors and other consultants. Observe what you like and dislike about them.

Step 4: Create the site. If you have the skills and inclination, you can save several thousand dollars or more by creating your own website. But unless you are an experienced Web designer, I suggest that you hire a professional. Ask your colleagues who they have used or look for sites you like and find out who designed them.

There are three basic skills a good Web designer should possess. Ideally, you will find someone with all three. First, he or she should be technically sound in terms of html coding and computer skills. You want the site to be able to function well no matter what type of computer or browser visitors are using.

Second, the designer should have a good sense of design (i.e., what will be friendly to the eye and fit the image you want to portray). The person should have a good sense of color, styles, fonts, and graphic design.

A third requirement for a good designer is that he or she must have experience advising consultants about how to market their services. A site that functions well and looks attractive is not enough. It needs to be able to lead you to new business. You will need advice about what should and should not be on the site in order to attract and interest the visitors you are seeking.

Talented Webmasters are usually not talented writers. You may need to write the first draft of the copy for your site and then hire a writer. A good writer will be able to tweak your words so that they sound professional and convey the appropriate image.

Here are a few suggestions for the content of your website:

◻ **Avoid splash pages, an initial page aimed at capturing the visitor's attention for a short time as a promotion or lead-in to the site.** These pages might look fancy, but they annoy many visitors. Most visitors will be willing to spend only a short period of time on your website. Splash pages needlessly cut into that time.

◻ **Good organization is the key to an effective website.** It should be easy for any visitor to quickly grasp how the site is organized and how they can quickly access the information in which they are interested.

- **Make it more than a brochure.** A website provides you with opportunity to do much more than just display static information. For example, it can include articles and papers that can be downloaded for free, audio and video content, the ability to search for information, links to other sites, a store where products can be purchased, forms that can be completed to begin receiving your newsletter, and, most importantly, a place where they can enter their contact information and request that you contact them.

- **Provide useful content.** If you want visitors to return to your website, it needs to provide useful information. Be careful, of course, not to give away your consulting services for free, but you do want to demonstrate to your visitors that you have expertise that is of value to them.

- **Avoid too much text.** Website visitors don't like to read a lot of information. Be brief when you describe your services.

- **Include testimonials.** Words from satisfied clients attesting to the value of your services are very powerful.

- **Keep the site fresh.** Update the site frequently by including new information. If your visitors see the same content month after month, there will be little reason for them to return to it.

- **Optimize your site.** Search optimization is the term used by website experts who know how to make your website appear at or near the top of search lists. Each search engine (e.g., Google, Yahoo!, etc.) uses different algorithms for deciding the order in which sites will appear on their results page of a search. For example, if you are a cost reduction expert for manufacturers, it would be great if your name appeared first on the search result list when someone conducts a Web search using the words "cost, reduction, manufacturing." Generally, if your site is visited frequently, is regularly updated, contains the appropriate key words, and is referred to often by other websites, you will appear relatively high in the search engine searches. Search engine optimizers are skilled at helping you to achieve these goals.

- **Make it easy for visitors to contact you.** Prominently provide your name, e-mail address, and other contact information.

Consider placing this information on every page. Some organizations don't provide their e-mail addresses because they fear they will be spammed or that their e-mail address will be used as a reply-to address by unscrupulous spammers. They instead have visitors submit their name on a form if they want to be contacted. Perhaps I am naive, but I prefer to display my e-mail address on my website and hope that spam filters will keep unwanted e-mail away from my in-box.

Advertise

Advertising can be an effective method for maintaining your visibility in the marketplace. It allows you to reach many more prospects than most other marketing techniques. It requires relatively little effort, although it can be costly. Here are a few basic principles to keep in mind:

- **Advertise in the right publications.** The size of the circulation of the publication isn't as important as whether the publication is read by your prospects. For example, if your target market is confined to your local region, it doesn't make sense to place an ad in a national magazine, which charges much more than local publications and may not help you reach more of your prospects. Similarly, if you target vice presidents of human resources, it makes more sense to advertise in the publication of the Society of Human Resource Management than it does to advertise in *BusinessWeek*. Not sure what your ideal prospects read? Ask your clients.

- **Advertise consistently.** You should view your advertising as a campaign. Budget permitting, it makes more sense to place an ad in every issue of a publication than only once in awhile.

- **Address benefits, not features.** Shy away from an overload of information about the features of your services. Instead, address a problem faced by your target market and the benefits you offer to alleviate the pain.

- **The advertisement should look professional.** Involve an experienced designer to help you with the look and feel of the ad. You want it to stand out from other ads and properly portray your image.

◻ **Placement within a publication is also important.** There are certain parts of a magazine that are read more often than others (e.g., the inside cover, back cover, and within the lead article). The publication can advise you about the best placement positions, but be prepared to pay more for the best.

◻ **Leverage articles you have published.** If you are publishing an article in a trade publication, consider placing an ad in the issue in which your article will appear. Ask that the ad be positioned within the same pages as your article. You may also be able to ask for ad space in lieu of payment for writing the article.

◻ **Provide all of your contact information.** Make it easy for readers to contact you via e-mail, phone, fax, or letter.

◻ **Provide an incentive.** Include in the ad an offer for something free that will increase the probability that a prospect will contact you. For example, offer a free initial consultation, a mini-session, or a feasibility assessment.

◻ **Purchase listings in resource guides.** Many professional associations provide print or Web Yellow Pages or directories. This is a place where members can search for services when they have a need. It often makes more sense to place ads or pay for a listing in these directories than to place ads in their publications.

◻ **Advertise on websites.** In many fields, prospects are more likely to see your ad if it appears on the home page of a newspaper, publication, or professional association. Web ads provide an immediate way for your prospects to learn more about you. When they click on the ad, they are transferred directly to your website. Websites that provide opportunities for advertising typically charge based on what page your ad appears (e.g., it usually costs more to be on the home page), the size of your ad, and how often it appears.

◻ **Advertise on search engines.** Search engines such as Google and Yahoo! provide services so that your ad appears on the search results pages that are displayed for certain key words you designate. For example, if you are a consultant who specializes in helping companies become more creative and innovative, you could buy an ad that would appear when someone searches using the key words "innovation, creativity, and consultant." You pay only when your ad is clicked. Some of the services also protect you from spending more than your budget by removing the ad once the allotted number of visitors have clicked on it.

◻ **Track the effectiveness of your ads.** Web ads and search engine ads provide you with a count of the number of clicks and then compute how this translates into sales. It is much more difficult to accurately assess the effectiveness of print advertisements, so make it a habit of asking your prospects how they heard about you. If you find over time that no one ever tells you they saw your print ad, consider pulling it.

Write Press Releases

Producing press releases is another method of marketing that provides the opportunity to maintain your visibility with a wide audience. Also called news releases, media releases, and press statements, these written announcements are mailed, faxed, or e-mailed to the editors of newspapers, magazines, websites, radio stations, and television stations for the purpose of announcing something of news value. For consultants, the major objective of a press release is to get mentioned as an industry expert in a publication read by your prospects. The reporter or editor may simply use the information in the release, or may call to interview you about the content, or may file it away in order to call you at a later date when they are writing a story in which you could appropriately be quoted.

The three steps involved in launching a press release campaign follow:

Step 1: Assemble a list of media contacts. Your first task in conducting a press release campaign is to gather the e-mail addresses, telephone numbers, or fax numbers of media contacts. Many newspapers, magazines, newsletters, and websites are looking for fresh ideas. Although some editors and writers ignore press releases, many do look through them. If they find your idea interesting, they will use the information or contact you.

It is important that you target the right types of news outlets. For example, if you are a marketing consultant for high-tech manufacturers, it probably doesn't make sense for you to send press releases to popular magazines such as *Oprah, Glamour,* or *Good*

Housekeeping. But if you are a consultant to the women's clothing industry, those magazines could be good candidates.

You can assemble a media list in one of the following ways:

- **Create it yourself.** Assembling your own list of media contacts can be a considerable amount of work, but it is inexpensive and may result in a more relevant list than you could ever purchase. The contact information, including e-mail addresses, of editors and writers is often listed on the masthead or on the same page that contains the copyright information. The e-mail addresses of writers are often displayed at the end of stories they write. Keep adding names and contact information to your master list as you read publications in your field. You can also find contact information in reference books available in most good libraries. In addition, you can scan the Web for publications in your field and search for contact information on their websites. Writers and editors frequently change jobs, so it is important that you keep your list current.

- **Purchase a list.** Another approach is to purchase a list of media contacts. There are many list brokers that sell such lists. Again, it is important that you make certain the list focuses on media outlets that are relevant to your consulting work.

- **Use a press release service.** For a fee, companies such as PR Newswire will distribute your press release to their list of media contacts.

Step 2: Prepare the press release. Editors are looking for news that will be of value to their readers. The fact that you landed a new client, moved your office, celebrated the anniversary of your fifth year in business, or doubled your sales probably won't interest them or their readers. Here are a few ideas that might:

- **Announce the results of a research study.** Summarize the key results and their implications.

- **Announce the release of your new book.** Be sure to present a few quotations that capture the essence of the content or message of the book.

◘ **Announce the results of a survey.** Editors love to cite statistics in their articles. Present the key results and conclusions of the survey in the news release.

◘ **Provide some insight based on your consulting expertise on a hot news topic.** This might include your thoughts on the results of an election, an escalation in a war, a new medical discovery, a spike in gasoline prices, a massive company layoff, or the bankruptcy of a major corporation.

Press releases are structured documents containing the following seven parts.

1. **Headline:** A statement that grabs the attention of the reader and briefly summarizes the news the release will present

2. **Contact:** Your name and contact information so that the writer can contact you to gather additional information

3. **Dateline:** The date of the release and the city and state where it originated

4. **Introduction:** The first paragraph, which should tell the reader who wrote the release, what it is about, where and when the news took place, and why the news is valuable

5. **Body:** The next paragraph or two, which provides more detail about the news and should include quotes from you about the news

6. **Brief bio:** Provides additional information about you

7. **Close:** Place three "#"symbols (###) to indicate the end of the release

Here are two sample press releases. The first release presents the results of my employee survey work, while the second is an announcement about an award won by my first book. The objective of the first was to continue to brand myself as an expert in the field of employee surveys. The objective of the second was to promote my book. Both were e-mailed to business editors of newspapers, magazines, radio stations, and television stations, and both resulted in stories and interviews about my work.

TO: Business Editors
SUBJECT: 60% of workers dissatisfied with pay, survey says.
FREE Report

FOR IMMEDIATE RELEASE

For Further Information Contact:
Bruce Katcher, Ph.D.
Email: BKatcher@DiscoverySurveys.com
Direct phone: 781-784-4367
URL: http://www.DiscoverySurveys.com

★　★

**Study Reveals that 6 out of 10 Employees Are Dissatisfied With
Their Pay**

Solutions to Top Three Issues Explained in FREE Report on the Web

★　★

Sharon, MA—February 12, 2010—Sixty percent of workers are dissatisfied
with the pay they receive from their employers, according to surveys conducted by Discovery Surveys, a management consulting firm specializing in
assessing employee opinions.

This result is based upon studies conducted in more than 70 organizations
during the past several years. More than 50,000 employees were surveyed
from a variety of U.S.-based manufacturing and service organizations.
Employees were asked whether they feel they are paid fairly compared to
others performing similar work in other organizations.

"Pay dissatisfaction often results in decreased motivation, decreased morale,
poor work quality, and increased turnover," says Dr. Bruce Katcher, an
Industrial/Organizational psychologist and author of the study. "The three
major sources of pay dissatisfaction are with the pay structure, the pay level,
and with merit increases." Of these three, says Katcher, "employees are least
satisfied with the link between their pay and their job performance."

In a report titled "Pay Dissatisfaction," that can be accessed at
http://www.discoverysurveys.com/articles/itw-001.html, Dr. Katcher offers
solutions for reducing these sources of dissatisfaction.

To receive free, monthly, e-mailed reports on other results from the employee surveys conducted by The Discovery Group, subscribe to the company's e-zine, "Improving the Workplace," at http://www.discover surveys.com/newsletter.htm.

# # #

TO: Business Editors
SUBJECT: Book named one of best business books of year.

FOR IMMEDIATE RELEASE

For Further Information Contact: Irene Majuk
Email: IMajuk@amanet.org
Direct phone: 212-903-8087

New York, NY—February 20, 2008—*30 Reasons Employees Hate Their Managers,* published by AMACOM, was recently named one of the best business books of the year by *strategy+business magazine,* a publication of Booz Allen Hamilton.

The book, authored by Dr. Bruce Katcher, an Industrial/Organizational psychologist, discusses why employees resent their managers and what managers can do about it. Each chapter discusses a common employee complaint and offers specific solutions. Chapter titles include:

We feel like slaves.
I'm afraid to speak up.
There are different rules for different people here.
Management doesn't listen to us.
There's no link between my pay and job performance.
Why don't they get rid of all the dead wood around here?

The book is based on studies conducted in more than 65 organizations during the past several years. More than 50,000 employees were surveyed from a variety of U.S.-based service and manufacturing organizations.

According to *OfficePRO Magazine,* "This book will open your eyes. Here's a glimpse of how employees view their management. The research in *30 Reasons Employees Hate Their Managers* will reveal exactly what you can do in your organization to attain higher productivity and more satisfied employees."

Wellesley, MA-based management psychologist Dr. Paul Powers said, "I'm not a bit surprised Dr. Katcher's book was picked as one of the best business books of the year. Every executive I gave it to devoured it."

For more information about the book including excerpts, visit: http://www.amanet.org/books/book.cfm?isbn=9780814409152.

To receive a sample copy of *30 Reasons Employees Hate Their Managers,* contact Irene Majuk, Publicity Director for AMACOM books at 212-903-8087 (IMajuk@amanet.org).

Also contact Irene Majuk to arrange a telephone, radio, or television interview, or you can contact Dr. Katcher directly at 781-784-4367 or BKatcher@DiscoverySurveys.com.

Bruce Katcher, Ph.D., is an Industrial/Organizational psychologist, consultant, speaker, and author. His firm, Discovery Surveys, conducts customized employee opinion surveys. He writes and speaks about how to improve the functioning of organizations by better managing employees.

# # #

Step 3: Distribute the press release. Some editors and reporters receive hundreds of press releases each day, so your competition for their attention may be fierce. In order to increase your odds of having it read, you will likely want to send your press release to many members of the media. E-mailing the releases is the least time consuming and least expensive option for this. You can use your own ISP and send the release in many small batches, or you could use an html e-mail distribution service to e-mail the press release all at once. Another option is to pay for a Web-based press release distribution service. A few news professionals still prefer faxed press releases.

After you have distributed the press release, make certain you are available to respond to phone calls or e-mails from reporters and editors. If anyone contacts you, it will probably be within the first or second day after you distribute the release.

Conduct Radio and TV Interviews

Radio and television interviews are another powerful way of marketing your services. Here are the three steps involved:

Step 1: Land the engagement. Radio and television interviewers look for interesting, newsworthy information to share with their listeners. Consultants gain interview opportunities by directly contacting the interviewers (or their production staff), submitting press releases to the program, or working through an agent, publicist, or marketing professional. A good publicist will already have developed relationships with interviewers.

My colleague Tom Kennedy, a former television and radio broadcaster, helps consultants and business executives prepare for media interviews (www.kennedygroupboston.com). He says, "It is much better for someone else to pitch your story to the media than for you to do it yourself. They will be able to speak in more glowing terms about you than you ever could do yourself. Also, they will prevent you from getting raked over the coals and make sure that your message is not distorted."

Tom also shares that it is important to research the media outlet (i.e., the radio or television interview program): "You need to find out about their audience so that you or your publicist can tell them how an interview with you will benefit their audience. You also need to be able to tell them your message in one sentence, emphasizing 'the hook' (i.e., what will get the attention of their listeners)."

Step 2: Prepare for the interview. Preparation for radio and television interviews is very important. You need to know who is going to interview you and what they might ask and to rehearse what you are going to say. Without proper preparation, the interview will be unfocused, your message will be unclear, and neither you nor your message will be remembered. Here are a few tips to help you prepare:

❑ **Listen to the interviewer ahead of time.** If the station is not in your area, you can often listen live or to past shows by visiting the station's website. Interviewing styles vary greatly, depending on the interviewer, the type of show, and the type of audience. For example, my publisher arranged for several radio interviews to help me promote my first book, *30 Reasons Employees Hate Their Managers*. A preacher from a small radio station in North Carolina conducted one of the interviews. His questions were very serious and addressed the key issue of the importance of managers and employees treating each other respectfully. His objective was to try to spiritually move his audience into bringing more humanity into the workplace. Another day, a pair of shock jocks interviewed me. They started the interview by saying, "We hate our boss. What can we do?" Their objective was purely to entertain their audience. Listening to these interviewers ahead of time helped me to anticipate the type of questions I would be asked.

◘ **Visualize the audience.** Your message needs to be focused on the listeners of the program, not you or the interviewer. Your delivery will be much more effective if you prepare by picturing the audience in your mind and imagining that you are delivering your message directly to them.

◘ **Be clear on your major message and themes.** Tom Kennedy says, "You need to think about what you want the audience to remember, and then say it during your introduction, conclusion, and several times in between. Limit yourself to only two or three major themes that you want to discuss, and prepare a story for each theme. Introduce each theme by saying something like, 'and let me tell you a story about that.'"

◘ **Send a set of sample interview questions ahead of time to the interviewer.** This will save them the time and trouble of having to develop their own questions. It also makes it much easier for you since you know what will be asked, although also be prepared for them to deviate from your questions.

◘ **Prepare someone to be a lifeline for you.** If you are going to be interviewed on a call-in show, have someone you know call in with a question you've prepared in advance.

◘ **Prepare stories.** Short stories, anecdotes, or quotes are extremely useful during radio or television interviews. A local newspaper once interviewed me for their feature called "Entrepreneur of the Week," which appeared in each Monday's business section. She came to my office armed with a pen, small notebook, and list of questions. I could see during the interview that she wasn't writing anything down. I guess my responses weren't that interesting to her. At one point, however, I blurted, "I would rather die than work for someone at a full-time job again." She quickly jotted that down and had the lead paragraph for her story. Interviewers (and audiences) appreciate anecdotes and provocative statements. Have several of them planned and well rehearsed. Keep a list of them by your side so you remember to use them while you are answering a question.

○ **Review your notes from prior interviews.** There is definitely a practice effect to good interviewing. I noticed that during the period when I was promoting my first book, the later interviews were much better than the earlier ones. My message was clearer. I included more stories. And most importantly, I made certain that the interviewer plugged my book. I took notes after each interview about what went well and what didn't. I also had colleagues listen to the interviews and provide me with feedback. Before each subsequent interview, I reviewed my notes. It helped a great deal.

○ **Confirm the details.** Most radio interviews these days are conducted via telephone rather than in the radio studio. Radio interviews are often set up by producers a month or more in advance. Make certain to confirm details, such as the date, time, who is going to initiate the call, who will be conducting the interview, and how long it will last. Schedules, interviewers, and even producers change frequently.

○ **Develop a point of concentration.** The media interview is a performance that you are giving for an audience. Prior to a performance, good actors focus on something that will help them to be more real in the moment. For example, they might choose a focus like "I really want to help the audience." Or they might adopt the focus "I am the expert on this topic." These types of concentration points will make your performance more believable to the audience.

Step 3: Conduct the interview. Here are a few tips to make telephone radio interviews more effective:

○ **Use a landline.** Old-fashioned landlines that directly connect to the handset are more reliable than cell phones or phones with wireless handsets.

○ **Turn off all noises.** Mute your computer, other telephones, and other electronic devices. Also make certain you are uninterrupted by visitors.

◻ **Warm up your voice.** Singing or saying vowel sounds just prior to the interview can help you prepare your voice.

◻ **Keep a glass of water nearby.** You never know when your mouth might dry up.

◻ **Stand up during the interview.** This will increase your energy level and enthusiasm. Speak slowly but enthusiastically.

◻ **Answer the questions, but make sure you address the key points you want to present.** It is important that you are responsive to the interviewer's questions, but you also want to make certain that you convey your major message and themes.

◻ **Don't say "umm" or "you know."** This may require practice ahead of time.

◻ **Use the name of the interviewer.** This will make you seem friendly and, at the same time, professional.

◻ **If you don't understand a question, ask for clarification.** Don't just ramble without being clear what you have been asked.

◻ **Be confident.** Remember, you are the expert.

◻ **Keep an eye on the clock.** If it is only going to be a five-minute interview, you want to make certain that you get across your major message and themes within that time. You also want to make certain that there is time for you to conclude properly.

◻ **Mention your contact information.** If the interviewer doesn't mention your company name, website, book, or contact information, then you need to do it.

◻ **Thank the host.** Make certain that you thank the host by name at the end of the interview.

Conclusion

The purpose of the four marketing techniques described in this chapter (maintaining a website, advertising, writing press releases, and conducting radio and television interviews) is to maintain your visibility among your outer ring of prospects and those who can refer you to prospects. Again, these include the many people who are outside of both your inner circle of contacts and your middle circle of known prospects. It is wise not to ignore them.

CHAPTER 11

Marketing Your Services Through Networking

My Uncle Richard retired many years ago from a successful retail photography business in South Orange, New Jersey, called Richard's Studio. He and his partner photographed individuals and families, weddings, and bar mitzvahs. When my uncle retired, he sold the business to his partner. The tricky part of the transaction was valuing the business. Like any business, it was worth much more than the dollar value of the assets (i.e., the building, fixtures, equipment, and accounts receivable). More importantly, it also had intrinsic value, such as the reputation the business enjoyed with its customers and in the community. Accountants call this *goodwill*.

As a consultant, your business has very few tangible assets. Your office equipment is probably worth only a few thousand dollars. Almost 100 percent of the value of your business is your goodwill, which consists of:

◘ Any ongoing business you maintain with clients

◘ The client trust you have developed, which makes them inclined to do business with you again

◻   Your client list

◻   Testimonials you have received from your clients

◻   The reputation you have established among prospects in the marketplace, which makes you the go-to person in their eyes should they have a need for your services

◻   The trust you have engendered among former coworkers and colleagues, who understand and value your work

◻   The trust you have developed within your personal and professional network, which makes them inclined to recommend your services to others

The Challenge

Like grapes on a vine, your network needs to be constantly watered or it will shrivel and die. Feed your network of friends, colleagues, former clients, and prospects by talking, writing, and meeting with them regularly. Otherwise, they may forget about you and not be there when you need them.

Maintaining contact with your network can be difficult, however, when your time is occupied by current clients, marketing, developing new service lines, and trying to maintain some semblance of work/life balance.

Solutions

This chapter discusses three strategies for keeping your network alive and well:

1. Maintain contact with your network
2. Develop relationships with service providers
3. Attend professional meetings

Maintain Contact with Your Network

Fifty-nine percent of The Consulting 200 said that maintaining contact with their network is the most effective approach they use to market their consulting services, making this far and away the most important of the 18 marketing strategies discussed in this book.

Do not just burrow in your office and hope you will receive telephone calls from qualified prospects. You've got to work hard at keeping up with your network, especially former clients who were pleased with your work. They are the best source of leads for new business. They can either engage you to conduct additional work or refer you to their colleagues. But if you maintain no contact with them, they may quickly forget about you.

Here is a three-step strategic process that can help you keep in contact with the most valuable members of your network:

Step 1: Identify your best contacts. These could include current clients, former clients, influential members of the business community, heads of professional associations in your area of expertise, well-connected fellow consultants, or friends. Limit the number of people on this list to a number you feel you can effectively manage. I try to limit mine to fifty.

Step 2: Select your networking methods. You will not necessarily use the same method for each person. Here are seven ways to touch members of your NETWORK:

N **Newsletter:** Your entire network should receive either your print or e-mail newsletter. It should be more than a commercial about your work and provide content that is useful and valuable to your network.

E **E-Mail:** Share information with network members, such as an article that you think they may find interesting or a link to a website that might be useful to them.

T **Telephone:** Call to make an introduction, share some important information, or to follow up on work you performed for them. Ideally, you will provide them with some value when you call. Asking for advice, asking a question, or asking a favor (e.g., a testimonial or an introduction) can also be useful approaches to keeping up with your network. Psychological studies based on the theory of cognitive dissonance have shown that when people do you a favor, they end up liking you more. Why? Because it would be inconsistent for them to do you a favor and not like you.

W **Work the crowd at professional meetings:** Make certain to sit next to your key network contacts or spend some time speaking with them.

O   Oral meetings: Chats over breakfast, coffee, lunch, dinner, and drinks are all possibilities.

R   Relax: Invite your key contact to a fun event, such as a concert, the symphony, or a ball game.

K   Kindness: Show them acts of kindness by sending birthday, holiday, or sympathy cards.

It is important that you use the approaches that you are comfortable with. Otherwise you won't consistently maintain contact with your network.

Step 3: Create a networking plan spreadsheet. Don't leave your networking to chance. If you do, connections may not happen often enough. Create a spreadsheet like the one in Table 11-1, with a row for each of the valuable members of your network and a column for each month. Fill up each cell with one or more of the seven networking techniques just described.

TABLE 11-1. A SAMPLE NETWORKING SPREADSHEET.

Key Member of Network	Jan	Feb	Mar	Apr	May	June
1. Harvey W.	N,W	N,T	N,R	N,O	N,K	N,R
2. Bob G.	N,E	N,T	N,K	N	N,E	N
3. Lila M.	N,T	N,E	N,E	N,K	N,E	N
4. Tracy R.	N	N	N,E	N	N,K	N
5. Don H.	N,E	N,O	N	N,E	N	N,K
6. Dave R.	N,T	N,O	N,T	N	N,E	N
7. Donna H.	N	N,T	N	N,T	N	N,E,T
8. Pam W.	N,W	N,O	N	N,O	N	N,O
9. Ginny R.	N,O	N,O	N,O	N,O	N,O	N,O
10. Mike M.	N,O	N,O	N,O	N,O	N,O	N,O

Follow your plan. Networking with your key contacts *must* become part of your regular routine. Each week transfer information from the spreadsheet to your daily to-do list. Maintaining contact with your network is critically important to your business. Invest the time, and you will see results.

Develop Relationships with Service Providers

Another approach to marketing your consulting services is to develop strategic relationships with other service providers who can refer business to you. The ideal candidates have frequent dealings with your target market. They must trust you and your work and believe that by recommending your services their clients will benefit, thus improving their relationship as a trusted adviser with them.

For example, Frank Mancieri, a partner at b2bcfo, (www.b2bcfo.com), provides financial management services to companies. He has developed referral arrangements with a banker, a human resources consultant, a consultant who serves on the board of directors for small to mid-size businesses, and a personal financial adviser. His goal and company strategy is for all of the partners to develop strategic relationships with other consultants, as well as attorneys and CPAs.

Consider which other professional service providers conduct business with your target market. As long as your services don't compete, you might be able to help each other by developing a strategic referral relationship.

Attend Professional Meetings

As an independent consultant, there is no watercooler where you can meet with other professionals to bounce ideas, seek advice, gain introductions, pick up insights, or just share friendly conversation. Conversations "around the watercooler" can lead to new business by expanding your network and learning about others who have needs you can address. It is, therefore, important that you push yourself to get out and interact with other professionals—to create your own watercooler.

There are three types of professional meetings that independent consultants should attend on a regular basis as part of their marketing strategy:

1. Professional meetings attended by your prospects
2. Professional meetings attended by fellow consultants
3. Professional meetings in your specific discipline

Attending professional meetings that are also attended by your prospects can be an ideal method for indirectly marketing your services. It is important that you appear at these meetings with the proper attitude and orientation. If you just stand around and pass out your business card to people you barely know, you will probably do more harm than good to your business. Instead, look for opportunities to help others by providing useful information or making introductions. Also, rather than talking about yourself, ask questions. People love to talk about themselves. If you are a good listener, you will be viewed as a worthy colleague.

The more targeted the professional group you join, the better. For example, if your target market is managers in manufacturing companies who use SAP, then instead of joining professional meetings attended by all types of managers, or even all types of managers in manufacturing, try to identify a meeting of manufacturers who use SAP. If you don't know what professional associations your prospects attend, ask your current clients.

Some professional associations are consultant-friendly, while some are not. Some forbid consultants from joining, serving on committees, or even attending meetings. I once sat in on a board meeting of a professional association that felt it had too many consultants attending their meetings, so they tried to reduce the number by raising the membership dues for consultants and not sending them annual renewal notices.

If you are attending business or professional meetings as a way to network with potential prospects, choose meetings that are ripe with prospects. Be wary of meetings where there are more consultants than prospects. Career consultant Ginny Rehberg uses the term *wood* to refer to those who can hire consultants and *woodchucks* for fellow consultants who are there to "gnaw" on the wood. She says, "You want to attend meetings with more wood than woodchucks. If there are too many woodchucks, stop attending those meetings."

Also make certain that you join an association in which there are ample opportunities for you to interact with prospects. For example, many national associations don't have local meetings. They may only hold a few meetings a year and require you to travel to attend them. If you attend meetings only occasionally, people you talked to at the last meeting may well have forgotten your name. Other associations may have a large membership and several meetings a week that are rarely attended by the same people. Such a scenario makes it difficult to develop strong relationships.

It is also important that the right level of people attend the meetings. The membership list of an association may look attractive because it contains senior people from major companies. But often those who attend the meetings are junior staff, who probably aren't in a position to hire you. Attend several meetings before you join to get a feel for the type of people who attend.

Your goal at professional meetings is to interact with prospects. Many associations provide ample opportunity for this type of interaction, while others do not. I once dropped my membership at a professional association because there were no opportunities to interact with prospects. The typical morning meetings consisted of a coffee hour from 7:30 to 8:00 AM that was attended almost exclusively by woodchucks. The wood slipped into the room just in time for the meeting that started promptly at 8:00. The seats were arranged auditorium style, allowing little opportunity for interaction among attendees. After listening to a speaker, there was a short midmorning coffee break that provided very little networking time. At the end of the meeting at noon, everyone immediately bolted. The association provided good content without good networking opportunities.

It is better to consistently attend the meetings of one association than to inconsistently attend the meetings of many. You need to become a known quantity. If you attend just once in a while, you will always feel like and be viewed as a stranger. People are reluctant to do business with strangers.

Most professional associations need help from volunteers, and that can become a good networking opportunity. Instead of volunteering for a task where you will work alone, try to volunteer for a committee or an activity that will put you in touch with members of the association or people thinking about joining. That is a good way for people to get to know you.

Find an association that has the right *esprit de corps*. Ideally, the meetings will have a friendly, professional feel. You want to be part of an association where people go out of their way to be helpful and share ideas. You may need to attend several meetings to get a sense of these underlying qualities, but it is important that you enjoy and feel comfortable at the meetings. Otherwise, joining the association probably won't help your business and certainly will not contribute to the all-important "fun factor."

Associations of professional consultants can also be a useful venue for marketing your consulting services. These organizations are established so consultants can meet to discuss topics such as marketing, sales, charging clients, and maintaining good relationships with clients. They also provide an opportunity for consultants to network with each other and to provide emotional support.

You may be wondering how networking with other consultants can help you land new business. I can personally point to hundreds of thousands of dollars of business that came my way as a direct result of attending meetings of one of my local professional consulting organizations, The Society of Professional Consultants (www.spconsultants.org). Consultants who target your market but who offer different types of services than you are in a position to introduce you to their clients, refer business to you, or bring you in on their projects. You can reciprocate by doing the same for them.

By attending these meetings, you will also learn about new approaches to marketing and sales and pick up other valuable information to help you improve your business. Think of these meetings as the watercooler you don't have in your own office.

A third type of meeting you should consider attending as a way of marketing your business are meetings of professionals in your specific discipline. For example, if you are a CPA, meetings attended by other CPAs will allow you to learn about the latest changes in tax law. If you are an organizational development professional, meetings attended by your colleagues will help you learn about the latest advances in your field.

By attending these meetings, in addition to learning the latest information, you will undoubtedly rub elbows with people who are in a position to use your consulting services or those who know people who can use your services.

Survey Results: Do You Enjoy Networking at Professional Meetings?

The majority of The Consulting 200 enjoy networking at professional meetings.

Percent	I enjoy socializing and networking at professional meetings.
62	Strongly agree or agree
26	Partly agree/Partly disagree
11	Disagree or strongly disagree

Conclusion

The most important asset of your consulting business is not your academic credentials, certifications, or professional experience. It is your goodwill, which consists of your relationships.

You need to be premeditated about preserving and growing your network by proactively keeping up with your contacts, developing and nurturing strategic relationships, and expanding your network through active participation in the appropriate professional associations.

CHAPTER 12

Selling Your Consulting Services

SHOULD HAVE KNOWN BETTER.

A colleague of mine referred me to Daniel, who conducts human resource consulting for municipalities. He wanted to respond to an RFP (request for proposals) issued by a county government in the Midwest to conduct an employee opinion survey, my specialty. He had the municipal experience I lacked, I had the survey experience he lacked, and together we believed we could put together a solid proposal. He also brought Mark, his partner based in California who also had extensive municipal experience, into the discussion.

I met with Daniel at a local diner to discuss the possibility of working together. He struck me as a nice guy, but I sensed that although he had the relevant experience, he was not a good listener. He talked nonstop about himself and asked me very little. I was left with a slightly negative impression, but I hoped it would pass and not influence our working relationship.

I then wrote the proposal, with Mark's assistance. It required a great deal of work, but it was for a two-year project and looked like a very promising opportunity. I was impressed with Mark, and it was easy to work with him. Mark and I spoke several times with the people at the county who had issued the RFP and they appeared to be impressed with our experience and our proposal.

Several weeks after we submitted the proposal, the county informed us that we were one of three finalists and asked us to meet with them to present our approach to their committee. Based on the several positive conversations we had had with them, we felt we had a good chance to win the business.

All three of us decided to attend the meeting. This was no small decision, since it required us each to pay for flights, meals, and an overnight stay. But we believed it was worth the investment.

I was a little worried about Daniel doing too much talking, as he had done when he and I had met. I wanted to make certain that he agreed to allow me to handle any questions about employee surveying and to let Mark handle most of the other questions. Daniel seemed to agree with that strategy.

We were invited into a classroom to meet the six-person committee. We sat at the front of the room, and the committee peppered us with questions about our proposal. *My worst fears were realized.* Daniel talked nonstop. He talked in circles and really didn't answer their questions. I tried to nudge him under the table, but he didn't respond. I knew that our chances of winning the contract were now slim.

A week later we learned that we lost the business to another firm. The reason—Daniel had totally alienated them. He had broken the first rule of selling. *He had not listened.*

The Challenge

Selling is a critically important part of starting and growing an independent consulting practice. If you can't sell, your business is sure to fail. It's not something you can delegate to others. But don't despair. Even if you've never been a salesperson, you can do it. It's not rocket science!

One of the most important principles about selling consulting services (or selling anything for that matter) is this: *Your prospects don't want to understand; they want to be understood.*

Prospects—and clients too—want to know that you have listened carefully to them and understand their problem and needs. You can talk until you are blue in the face about your experience, your approach, and why you are the right person for the work, but what will impress them most is that you have listened to them, asked good questions, and understood their situation. This, in a nutshell, is the key to selling.

Why do consultants fail to listen? Here are a few reasons:

- **They want to strut their stuff.** Consultants are eager to tell the prospect about all their relevant experience. The problem is that the more the consultant talks, the less opportunity the prospect has to speak.

- **They come to the sales meeting with their mind already made up about what the prospect needs.** Many consultants are skilled at solving one particular problem or using one particular methodology. They are like hammers looking for nails. No matter what the client's problem, they will attempt to use the approach they are comfortable implementing. So instead of asking the client about their problem, they make assumptions about what is needed and fail to listen.

- **They appear too eager for the business.** Successful consultants act as though they are independently wealthy and don't need the business. This is far more attractive to the prospect then a consultant who begs for work.

- **They are anxious.** When consultants are anxious during sales meetings, they try to cover up their anxiety by talking too much. This interferes with their ability to listen to the prospect.

Solutions

Some basic sales strategies and techniques follow. They may require you to remove yourself from your comfort zone, but I strongly encourage you to try them all.

Talk with the Decision-Maker, Not the Gatekeeper

Most consultants are dead in the water before sales meetings even begin. The reason: They are talking to the wrong person. If you talk to a gatekeeper, he or she can only say "No" and must consult with others before saying "Yes." You want to do your best to make certain from the outset that you are talking with the decision-maker. Before the meeting, ask the person you will be meeting with if he or she has the authority to reach an agreement with you. You may not be able to meet with the decision-maker right away, but that needs to be your goal.

In a Competitive Situation, Try to Arrange to Be the Last Consultant to Meet with the Prospect

Ideally, you are providing a unique service and have no competition, but that is rarely the case. Let's say your contact telephones you to invite you to discuss working with his company and says that you are one of four firms that have been invited. He tells you that they will be meeting with people Monday morning, Monday afternoon, Tuesday morning, and Tuesday afternoon. Which appointment would you choose?

Before you answer this question, I would like you to participate in a short exercise. Please read the numbers below slowly, one at a time, from left to right:

74, 61, 96, 25, 18, 48, 57, 82, 65, 43, 38, 62, 84, 73, 68, 37, 41, 29, 27, 11, 12

Quickly, turn the page of this book so that you can no longer see the numbers and write down as many as you can remember. No peeking!

If you are like the vast majority of people, you remembered more numbers at the beginning and end of the list than in the middle. This is a well-known memory phenomenon called the *serial position effect*. Items at the beginning and end of the list are remembered better than those in the middle.

Based on this information, you would be better off conducting your sales appointment with your prospect Monday morning or Tuesday afternoon. But Monday morning can be the kiss of death.

Pretend for a moment that you are an Olympic diver about to enter the final round of competition. You are assigned to dive first. Your dive is perfect. Guess what! They are not going to give you a "10." They need to leave room for a performance that may be even better. And they haven't calibrated their judging based on the excellence of the divers.

Prospects do something similar during sales meetings. During the first meeting, they are not certain of the caliber of the consultants and don't really know the questions to ask. They tend to compare each consultant to those they have already met. At each meeting they ask different questions, gradually zeroing in on what's important to them.

You want them to ask you *all* their questions and zero in on you. Of course, you may have no say in the matter, but if you have a choice, choose to be the last consultant with whom they meet.

While I was working for a large international benefits consulting firm, a Fortune 500 company decided to put their pension and actuarial work out for bid. It sent an RFP to all of the major benefits consulting firms, including mine. The work was valued at several million dollars. My firm put all of their best actuaries from around the country to work on the proposal.

One day the savvy new business development person at our firm received a call from the company saying that we were one of four finalists and were invited to bring our team of actuaries to discuss their proposal. The company representative said, "We are meeting with firms two weeks from now on Thursday and Friday. Which day would you like to come in?" The new development person quickly responded, "Friday afternoon." The reply was, "Sorry, that's already taken."

The development person had to think fast. He said, "Let me check everyone's schedule and get back to you." The next day, he decided to take a risk. He called back and said, "I checked with our team, and several people will be out of the country that week. Would it be possible to meet with you on the following Monday?" The representative of the company checked with *his* team and agreed. To make a long story short, my firm met with them last (i.e., on Monday) and eventually won the business.

Arrive at the Sales Meeting Fully Prepared

Proper preparation is crucial. Find out everything you can about the company. Visit their website. Search the Web for the latest news about them. Reach out to your network to find out what they know about the company. Ask colleagues if they are familiar with the person you will be meeting with.

Prepare an agenda for the meeting. You may want to keep the agenda to yourself, although in some situations it may make sense to share it with your prospect. It will show that you are organized and will keep the meeting on track.

Bring a list of questions based on your research of the company. They should also be designed to get your prospect to articulate their pain (i.e., their problem or what needs to be solved).

Bring your calendar in case other meetings will be scheduled or they are ready to schedule the beginning of the project. Most importantly, bring a notepad so that you can take notes during the meeting. Prospects like when consultants take notes. It means that the consultant is treating everything they say seriously and is trying hard to understand their situation.

Establish Chemistry

The success of the sales meeting is all about chemistry. Try to develop open, friendly, and sincere rapport with your prospect. Here are some tips to help you establish successful chemistry with your prospects:

◻ **When you first meet, look the prospect straight in the eye** as you firmly shake hands and introduce yourself by name.

◻ **Listen carefully to the pronunciation of their name.** Use it occasionally during the meeting. If you have trouble remembering names, write it down immediately. This is particularly important if you are meeting with more than one person at a time. You want to make certain that when you say good-bye, you use everyone's name.

◻ **Begin with a little small talk.** Perhaps take note of the handsome family picture on the desk, the memorabilia on the shelf, the neatness of the office, or the weather. This helps to break the ice.

◻ **Maintain eye contact as much as possible.** Although you will be taking notes, it is important to maintain eye contact. If you are

---

Survey Results: Sales Training Is Highly Recommended.

About half of The Consulting 200 has attended formal sales training classes and half have not, but the majority (i.e., 62 percent) would recommend it for new consultants.

I have taken formal sales training.

Percent	
47	Strongly agree or agree
12	Partly agree/Partly disagree
50	Disagree or strongly disagree

I would recommend that new consultants take formal sales training.

Percent

62	Strongly agree or agree
29	Partly agree/Partly disagree
9	Disagree or strongly disagree

looking directly into the sun, that will be difficult, so if there is a window in the room, make certain you are seated with the sun to your back.

- **Keep your energy level high.** Be enthusiastic as you speak, and exude energy. Sit at the edge of your seat so that you don't become too relaxed or sleepy.

- **Be as genuine and forthright as possible.** This will help you to connect with the prospect.

Establish Ground Rules and Expectations at the Beginning of the Meeting

It is important that you try to take a little bit of control over the meeting by clarifying their time frame and expectations. Here are some ways to achieve this:

- **Ask first how much time they have reserved for the meeting.** Then you can pace your questions accordingly and bring the meeting to a proper close.

- **Ask them to confirm your understanding of what will happen during the meeting.** For example, you might say something like, "My expectation is that during this meeting I will ask you questions to learn more about your business and the problems you are facing, and you will ask me questions to learn about my work and how I might be able to help you. At the end of our time together, we will decide the next steps, such as our working together or my presenting you with a plan of action in writing. Is this your expectation as well?"

Think Ahead to the Proposal

Ideally, you won't need a proposal because your prospect will ask you at the end of the meeting, "When can you start and where do I send the check?" Unfortunately, it doesn't often play out that way. You will probably be asked to submit a proposal, especially if you are competing with other firms. Your most important task during the meeting is to gather all of the information you need to put together the proposal.

Use Active Listening Techniques

As previously mentioned, listening is the key to a successful sales meeting. You need to learn in their own words about their pain and what they would like accomplished. Here are several techniques to help you become a better listener:

◻ **Open-ended questions:** Ask questions that require full paragraph responses rather than one-word answers. For example, "What types of problems are you encountering with your new marketing campaign?" or "How have you tried to address the problem?" Avoid questions like, "What is your sales revenue?" or "How many years has the company been public?"

◻ **Follow-up questions:** Probe further by asking questions that follow up on the responses of your prospect. Questions can be as simple as, "Tell me more about that," or "Can you please elaborate on that?"

◻ **Restatements:** Simply restating what your prospect has just said is an effective technique for stimulating the prospect to elaborate. For example, if your prospect says, "We are having trouble retaining our junior accountants in the controller's office," you could respond, "You are having trouble retaining junior accountants in the controller's office." This may seem absurd, but it is effective.

◻ **Reflections:** This is a similar technique by which you identify an emotion, label it, and feed it back to your prospect. For example, if the prospect appears to be frustrated or angered by the lack of cooperation from the sales department, you might say something like, "The lack of cooperation from the sales department seems to be frustrating you." This will encourage the prospect to speak more about that issue, as well as demonstrate that you understand his feelings and his words.

◻ **Nonverbal listening:** In addition to maintaining eye contact, it is important that you nod your head and say things like "Uh-huh" to acknowledge that you have heard what has just been said.

◻ **Silent pauses:** After you ask a question, wait for a response. Avoid the nervous tendency to fill gaps in the conversation yourself. Wait until your prospect fills the void.

◻ **Interpretations:** Periodically, try to interpret what the prospect has said. For example, if they say that sales are low in the New York office and there have been a lot of management changes in that office, you could say something like, "It sounds like there have been many challenges in the New York office." Then wait and see if the prospect agrees and elaborates further.

Ask About Challenges

One technique that has been very valuable to me over the years is to ask prospects what challenges they anticipate the project will face. This question forces the prospect to voice any skepticism, reservations, or doubts they have about moving forward. Then make certain to address these reservations at the meeting and in your proposal.

Ask About the Economic Value of the Results

Ask a question such as, "If this problem were solved, how much money per year would your firm save or earn?" The answer will help your prospect understand the value of your services. It will also help you to price the project based on the value you will provide rather than how much time you will spend doing the work.

Ask About Competition

Do not be afraid to ask if you are competing with other firms. They may tell you valuable information such as the names of the firms and what the other firms have proposed. Also ask if there are things about the other firms that are particularly attractive to them. This information can be invaluable because it will enable you to respond to any specific concerns they may have about you.

Ask About the Budget

Also, don't be afraid to ask if they have a budget set aside for this work and how much it is. They probably will not give you a specific dollar amount, but if they do, you can quickly tell them whether you can do the work for that amount or whether you will need to modify the approach you may have already discussed with them.

Go for the Close

As the allotted time for the meeting is running out, say something like, "I want to thank you for inviting me in today and telling me about your company and what you would like accomplished. Based upon what you need, and what I can provide, it sounds like we have a pretty good match. Would you agree?"

Your prospect may not be able or willing to answer this question, but if they have objections, this is where they may emerge. They may say something like, "Well, we were really looking for a firm with more experience in our industry." In that case, you can give their concerns your best shot and talk about your relevant experience. If you don't ask, you won't realize their objections, and you will have no chance to respond to them.

Do not be too eager, however. You want to be enthusiastic, so it is a subtle balance to weigh. Acting like you are not desperate for the business will often make you seem more, rather than less, attractive to them.

If they say that they are planning to meet with other firms, ask them if you can call them or come back so that you can address any other questions or issues that arise. Tell them that this will enable them to compare apples to apples.

Before You Leave, Review Their Expectations Again

Ask your prospect the next steps in the process. For example, would they like you to submit more information, come back to meet others in the organization, or write a proposal? Here are some things you should do if they say they want you to write a proposal:

◻ **Tell them what will be in the proposal by reviewing the approach you have already discussed with them.** Then ask if they agree with what you plan to write.

◻ **Run the price by them or provide them with a range.** Ask them if that is within their budget.

◻ **Tell them that you would like to come back and discuss the proposal with them.** Try to schedule a date for that meeting before you leave.

After the Meeting, Don't Chase

One of the major frustrations consultants experience is chasing after prospects. Follow through after the meeting by sending your proposal and then call to discuss it or to schedule another meeting. But if they don't respond, do not call over and over again. Prospects know how to get in touch with you. Appearing overanxious will only hurt your cause. Spend your energy looking for new prospects rather than chasing down prospects that have gone cold.

Conclusion

If you are going to succeed in this business, you will have to learn how to sell. The most important skill you need to acquire to make sales is the ability to listen. Your technical skills and experience are important, of course, but they are actually secondary to your ability to sell yourself once you get in front of a qualified prospect.

Just going with the flow at a sales meeting will probably not land you the sale. You need to prepare properly and have a step-by-step plan for how you are going to approach the sales situation. You need to know ahead of time:

- How you are going to begin the meeting
- What you are going to ask
- How you are going to discover the real pain your prospect is experiencing
- How you are going to respond to objections
- How you are going to learn the budget and value they attach to the work
- How you are going to close the sale

Dedicate yourself to becoming a student of sales. Selling is one of the oldest professions. There are a wealth of books, seminars, and workshops on the topic. Join a sales and marketing association so that you can learn from other salespeople. Talk to fellow consultants about their approach.

You don't have to be dishonest or manipulative to be a good salesperson, but you do need a plan. That strategy should include getting your prospects to talk about the pain they are experiencing, listening rather than trying to talk your way through the sales meeting, and closing the sale.

CHAPTER 13

Writing Proposals That Lead to Business

M ANY YEARS AGO, while I was completing graduate school, I worked for a "beltway bandit." This is the unaffectionate term for the hundreds of consulting and contracting firms located on Route 495 surrounding Washington, DC, that do much of the work of the federal government. The seven-person firm I worked for conducted human resource consulting work for government agencies.

My job was to write proposals. It was a lonely, time-consuming, and unrewarding job. Four times a week the federal government published a small newspaper called the *Commerce Business Daily*. Each issue contained hundreds of RFPs, abbreviated in the form of short paragraphs that briefly described work that different agencies of the government wanted a consulting firm to perform. My boss would scan the listings and choose those that he thought we could possibly win. He then requested the full RFPs from the agencies.

The RFPs were typically one-hundred-page documents containing a number of boilerplate sections, including various requirements that bidders had to satisfy, such as affirmative action policies, proof of workman's compensation insurance, and business certifications. Somewhere embedded deep inside the document were a few pages that described the actual consulting work to be performed, typically called the statement of work.

My job was to respond to the RFP by writing a detailed proposal. This was an arduous task, typically requiring at least forty hours of work. There were many challenges to overcome.

For one thing, it was very competitive. Typically, at least a dozen other firms also planned to respond to the RFP. The proposal would be scrutinized by a committee and evaluated based on a set of standard criteria that were listed in the RFP. However, most of the RFPs were "wired." That is, the agency knew ahead of time to whom they were probably going to award the contract. They published the RFP because the law required them to do so. Everyone else who responded to the RFP was just wasting their time.

In fact, often the beltway bandits that responded to the RFP and eventually won the work had written the RFP in the first place. This was an illegal but standard practice in some agencies. The firms carefully wrote the RFP in such a way that they would be the only logical firm to do the work because of their experience or work on the original phase of the project.

Another challenge was that the statement of work was often unclear, disorganized, and contained contradictory information. It was usually unclear why the agency wanted the work conducted (i.e., the real objectives and the pain that needed to be reduced). Furthermore, it was almost impossible to gain much clarity about the objectives or the statement of work. We were not allowed to call the contact person to ask questions, and meeting with the contract monitor was strictly forbidden. Our questions about the statement of work had to be submitted to the contract monitor, who would answer the questions in writing. The problem was that the questions *and* responses were sent to everyone who had requested a copy of the RFP. So if you came up with good questions that would show your expertise and insights and help you write a winning proposal, every other proposer would also have access to the answers.

Clients hire people they trust and respect. But there was no way to establish meaningful contact or rapport with the decision-makers. The committee merely looked at a stack of proposals and tried to compare them on the technical merits of the proposal, the experience of the firm, and, of course, the price.

Price was a major issue. The agencies rarely provided any information about their budget or what the work was really worth to them. Also, the agencies were often legally obliged to award the contract to the lowest bidder that met the technical and experiential qualifications. This often left little room for the firm to make a profit to support people like me, a lowly proposal writer.

You only received one shot. There was no give and take, no opportunity to submit a preliminary proposal and then discuss it with the contract monitor, and no negotiation. You wrote the proposal, priced it, sent it off, and then just prayed that your firm would be selected.

My boss, a "glass-is-half-full" kind of guy, said it was just a numbers game. He said, "The more proposals we write, the more we will win." The bad news was that we didn't win many. The good news was that as long as we did win a few, I had job security. But this meant that I would have to keep writing many boring proposals, with a low probability of any one of them leading to sale.

The Challenge

Writing proposals can be a daunting and frustrating experience. Knowing when to write and when not to write a proposal is very important. Assuming you have the technical know-how and experience to do the work, you want to avoid writing proposals if:

- You haven't had the opportunity to meet with the prospect face-to-face ahead of time to build trust and rapport.
- You haven't had any contact with the real decision-maker.
- The prospect has shown no signs that they are interested in working with you.
- You don't have a good understanding of the pain the prospect is feeling or the objectives of the work.
- You don't know how the decision will be made.
- You are competing against a firm that has an inside track on winning the work.
- You have no idea what price your prospect has in mind.
- The probability of winning the work is low.

Solutions

Some recommendations to consider when writing proposals follow.

Write Each Proposal from Scratch

One size does not fit all. The proposal should be customized to fit the needs, language, and style of your prospect. If you merely cut and paste from proposals you have written in the past, it will read that way to the prospect. It will seem impersonal and not specifically directed to them. For example, wouldn't you use different language if you were writing a proposal to conduct strategic planning for a new manufacturing division of a Fortune 500 company versus a small nonprofit charity?

Adopt a positive, upbeat tone. The proposal should communicate to your prospect that you understand their problem and are confident you can solve it.

Use definitive language. Throughout the proposal say, "I will" or "We will," as opposed to "We can" or "We would."

Include the right amount of detail. It is important that you provide sufficient detail so prospects know what you plan to do, but not so much detail you bore them. The proposal will serve as your contract with the client. It therefore needs to include enough detail so that it is clear to the prospect what is included in the price and what would be beyond the proposal's scope.

Include Seven Sections in Your Proposals

Your proposal must be well organized and easy to read. Most importantly, it should clearly demonstrate that you listened carefully to what was said during your initial meeting and understand your prospect's situation. The proposal should include the following step-by-step approach that you will use to solve your prospect's problem and that addresses both the timing and the cost of the project.

1. Cover letter of memo. The cover letter should briefly state why you are writing and very briefly explain the content of the proposal. The first paragraph might go something like this: "It was a pleasure meeting you yesterday and learning about the XYZ Corporation. I would welcome the opportunity to help you. This letter outlines my understanding of the situation, the approach I will take, the timing, and the associated costs. In the Professional Fees section, I have provided several options for how we can work together."

If you are submitting a long letter or proposal, you might briefly summarize in a paragraph or two what makes you unique.

Instruct your prospect how to consummate the deal by saying something like, "If you agree to the approach and terms outlined in this proposal, please sign the signature page and fax it back to me."

Conclude the letter with a call to action. Say that you will call to follow up next week, or say if you haven't heard from them in a week or so, you will call.

2. Background and objectives. This first section of your proposal is key. This is where you prove that you really understand their situation. Try to use many of the actual words they used when talking to you. Here are the basic topics to include in this section:

- **The problem:** The first paragraph of this section might begin with the words, "I understand that ..." The paragraph should summarize their needs, their pain, and what work they want performed and why.

- **What has been tried:** The next paragraph can include a summary of what they have tried to do in the past to solve the problem and the results, or lack of results, they achieved.

- **The objectives:** The third paragraph might begin with something like, "You would, therefore, like to _____." This is where you briefly summarize their objectives and what they want you to do for them.

- **The challenges:** The paragraphs that follow should focus on the possible challenges the project might encounter, such as limited time, lack of cooperation of managers, resistance from employees, etc. Also, briefly mention how you plan to overcome these challenges if they occur.

- **Summation:** A paragraph should also be included that offers an overview of what is to be gained, such as, "The approach I have outlined below has been designed to meet these objectives and overcome these challenges."

- **Results:** In addition, the tangible results the client will receive from your work should be highlighted. It is important that you talk about the money or time that they will save, the increase in quality they will achieve, or the additional revenue they will receive as a result of your work.

▢ **Biographical information:** Finally, the section should end with a few brief paragraphs about you and your relevant experience. For example, be sure to mention the other firms for which you have successfully solved similar problems.

3. Approach. This section should include a step-by-step summary of the approach you plan to take. Map it out in enough detail so that your client understands your methodology, but not so much detail that it becomes tedious. This section shows the prospect that you are organized, will be able to take control, and will guide them easily through the process. Each step should begin with an action-oriented verb. For example, "Step 1: Conduct Planning Meeting"; "Step 2: Prepare Draft Communications."

4. Timing. Include a paragraph about how long the project will take to complete. For example: "The work described above can be completed in approximately eleven to twelve weeks." You might also want to include a table, such as Table 13-1, that makes the timing more specific:

TABLE 13-1. SAMPLE PROJECT SCHEDULE TO INCLUDE IN A PROPOSAL.

Project Step	Timing
Step 1: Conduct Planning Meeting	Week of Aug. 7
Step 2: Prepare Draft Communications	Week of Aug. 7
Step 3: Conduct Focus Groups	Aug. 14 or Aug. 15
Step 4: Design Survey	Aug. 7 – Aug. 18
Step 5: Post Survey to Web	Aug. 18 – Aug. 31
Step 6: Administer Survey	Sept. 5 – Sept. 15
Step 7: Conduct Data Analysis	Sept. 18 – Sept. 29
Step 8: Prepare Executive Summary Report	By Oct. 9
Step 9: Conduct Oral Presentation(s)	Week of Oct. 16
Step 10: Deliver Employee Results Report	By Oct. 24

5. Fees and expenses. This section of the proposal should outline the fees for the project, as well as which expenses are included and which are additional.

You can provide one number for the project—a range (e.g., $10,000–$15,000)—or several options. Providing options is a good way to provide flexibility in your fees. It will enable your prospect to choose whether they want you to conduct the work just as you proposed it, less than you proposed, or more. You need to make it clear what is included and what is not included at each price point. Table 13-2 shows the type of chart I often include in my proposals:

TABLE 13-2. SAMPLE CHART FOR THREE OPTIONS TO INCLUDE IN A PROPOSAL.

PROJECT STEP	Option A	Option B	Option C
Step 1: Conduct Planning Meeting	In person	In person	Via telephone
Step 2: Prepare Draft Communications	Yes	Yes	No
Step 3: Conduct Focus Groups	Yes	Yes	No
Step 4: Design Survey	Yes	Yes	Yes
Step 5: Post Survey to Web	Web	Web	Paper surveys No Web
Step 6: Administer Survey	Yes	Yes	Client
Step 7: Conduct Data Analysis	Up to 30 lines in data comparison report	Up to 20 lines in data comparison report	Up to 15 lines in data comparison report
Step 8: Prepare Exec. Summary Report	Yes	Yes	No
Step 9: Conduct Oral Presentation(s)	Two	One	One
Step 10: Prepare Employee Results Report	Yes	No	No
PROFESSIONAL FEES	**$19,500**	**$16,500**	**$10,500**

You should then also include a paragraph or two about which expenses are included in your fee and which are additional. For example, I typically say, "Out-of-pocket expenses for travel, postage, and printing are additional and will be billed to you as they are incurred."

Next, include a payment schedule. For example, you might want to charge one-third at the beginning of the program, one-third after you have presented a specific deliverable, and one-third at the end. Alternatively, you might charge half up front and half midway through the program. Another option is to charge the full amount prior to beginning the project. Some consultants offer to discount their fees for full payment up front.

6. Client lists, testimonials, and references. Including these in your proposal can help boost your credibility. It may not be necessary if you know the prospect well or if you have conducted work for them in the past. However, even if you know one person well, others involved in the decision may need more convincing about your experience. I recommend including a list of clients, testimonials, and references if you know that your proposal is going to be compared to others, if this is your first attempt to do work for this prospect, or if you have a list of clients, testimonials, and references that will probably be viewed as credible and relevant.

7. Signature page. Include a page that provides a place for your prospect to sign and date your proposal and one to indicate which option they have selected. Ask them to fax back a signed copy of the signature page so that the project can begin immediately.

Conclusion

Writing a proposal should be the culmination of meaningful interactions you have had with the client by which you have gained a good understanding of their pain and their objectives. Ideally, you will already have begun to build trust and talked through the methodology, timing, and cost. The proposal will then be a written restatement of what you have already agreed upon in principle.

In your proposal, you want to demonstrate that you understand their situation and have a solution to their problem and the expertise to achieve the proposal's objectives. You must also make clear the tangible results that you will achieve.

PART 3

Keeping the Gas Tank Filled

CHAPTER 14

Delivering Tangible Results

S EVERAL YEARS AGO DEBORA BLOOM, who heads Debora Bloom Associates, asked me to help her develop a proposal and to be part of a consultant team working for a large civil engineering construction project in the northeastern United States. As diversity consultants, she and her associates provide consulting and training services to organizations to help them build inclusive, respectful, and productive workplaces.

This large government-funded construction project had a staff of nearly a thousand employees, plus hundreds of contractors. Although the metropolitan area in which the project took place is quite diverse, the construction project's staff had limited diversity in terms of race, ethnicity, and gender. The limited representation of people of color and of women was reflective of the construction industry at the time. Although no specific discriminatory incidents prompted the request for diversity training, senior staff, the human resources director, and the organization's Diversity Council all wanted the work environment to become more inclusive. They were seeking diversity training as a useful complement to other EEO/affirmative action activities and to contribute to better community relations.

Because of the project's high profile, and because of the large amount of taxpayer money involved, the organization also wanted to be able to prove that the diversity training worked. They wanted a training program that could make a difference and demonstrate tangible results. They wanted proof that the time and effort spent on diversity training improved working relationships within the workforce. The client was willing to fund the evaluation process. The project had an assessment phase, a training phase, and an evaluation phase.

That's where I came in. Debora asked me to measure the effectiveness of the training she was planning to conduct. The training was designed to increase employee understanding of diversity issues, elevate appreciation of differences, and help participants develop personal plans to improve how they managed diversity in the workplace. The training took place at all levels of the organization, with slight program modifications depending on whether the participants were individual contributors, managers, or executives.

In our proposal, we told the client that we would conduct a pretest before the training, a post-test immediately following the training, and a follow-up test two to three months later. Testing was designed to measure whether or not the training program had the intended effect of improving awareness, understanding, and respect for differences in the workplace.

Although we were optimistic that the program would be effective, our consulting team did not really know whether the short half-day training program the client had requested would be sufficient to meet their objectives. We were targeting soft behaviors, as opposed to more easily measurable issues such as cost reduction or productivity improvements.

I developed a brief, anonymous assessment tool that asked employees to honestly rate themselves on how well they were cooperating with people of different genders, sexual orientation, and ethnic, racial, and religious backgrounds. The construction project's employees attended the program in small groups and, as planned, were tested before each training session began, immediately afterwards, and then again three months later. We then analyzed the results to determine if there had been any significant improvements.

We were quite pleased to learn that the ratings improved dramatically between the pre-test and the follow-up post-test. Employees reported that they were now treating each other more respectfully and were working together more effectively. We had met the objectives of the program and delivered the tangible results our client was seeking.

The Challenge

Providing clients with value (i.e., tangible results) is the challenge all consultants constantly face. Otherwise, why would someone hire you? Here are four reasons you need to constantly focus on delivering tangible results to your clients:

1. **To gain repeat business:** It is much easier to sell services to clients who trust and respect you than to prospects with whom you have no relationship. The way you gain their respect is by providing tangible results.

2. **To land referrals:** Satisfied clients will be much more willing to refer you to other organizations.

3. **To continue to improve:** Measuring the effectiveness of your work will help you to continue to fine-tune your consulting skills.

4. **To strengthen your marketing efforts:** Your marketing will be much more effective if you can boast in your letters and literature and on your website about the tangible results you have achieved for your clients, rather than only a list of the services you delivered.

There is an important distinction between delivering services and providing value. Conducting a training program or a survey, developing a new sales incentive program, hiring a new employee, preparing a marketing brochure, coaching a senior executive, or developing a strategic plan are all examples of services. But these deliverables are only important to clients if they provide results.

Which of the following marketing statements is more powerful?

◻ Developed a sales training program for a national financial services company to teach the sales force how to sell a revamped retirement annuity product to existing customers

◻ Increased sales by 25 percent in the first year by training the sales force how to sell a revamped retirement annuity product to existing customers

In the first bullet, the end result is the development of a training program. In the second bullet, the end result is a sales increase of 25 percent. The second statement is obviously a more powerful reason for someone to hire you.

There are essentially only two ways to provide value for organizations. You can help your client make money, or you can help your client save money. Virtually all consulting objectives directly or indirectly fall into these two categories of value. Table 14-1 shows some common consulting objectives and how they correspond either directly or indirectly to these two ways of providing value.

TABLE 14-1. THE TWO MAJOR WAYS CONSULTANTS PROVIDE VALUE FOR CLIENTS.

Consulting Objective	The Real Underlying Objective
Increase sales	
Increase donations	
Increase membership	
Increase readership	
Improve quality	
Hire new employees	
Improve employee morale	**Help the organization make money**
Increase employee motivation	
Improve customer satisfaction	
Reduce complaints	
Improve senior managers' teamwork	
Improve managers' effectiveness	
Reduce costs	
Increase productivity	
Increase efficiency	
Reduce time needed to produce products	
Reduce time to market	
Streamline processes	
Retain customers	**Help the organization save money**
Improve employee cooperation	
Improve employee communication	
Reduce employee turnover	
Reduce accidents	
Reduce errors	
Avoid the cost of fines and penalties	
Comply with government regulations	

Solutions

Three strategies follow that will help ensure that you provide tangible results to your clients.

Probe for the Pain

It is your job to focus your prospects on the economic value of the work you can provide them: how it will help them solve a real problem and how you will be able to provide them with tangible results. If your prospects experience no "pain" or believe they have no real pressing need for your service, you are unlikely to win the business. If you are hired, you will be unlikely to provide them with tangible value.

Sometimes prospects have a real need for your services, but they don't understand their own pain or have difficultly articulating why they may want you to perform a particular consulting service. Here are a few reasons why this might be the case:

- *Just following orders:* Their boss asked them to hire a consultant without communicating the reason why. Their real goal is to please their boss, not provide value to their organization.

- *Running on autopilot:* They routinely ask for the same service each year but have lost track of how it provides them with value.

- *Conforming to what others have done:* They are interested in the consulting service because they think everyone else (i.e., other organizations) does it, so they should too.

- *Failure to see the big picture:* They have a short-term, myopic view of their situation and haven't really thought about how the service will help the organization in the long run.

Help Your Prospects Think in Dollars and Cents

It is your responsibility to get your prospects to think about the economic value of the work you can provide for them. Ask them questions such as:

- How could this work make your organization more profitable?

- How much money could this work save your organization?

- What is the risk, in dollars and cents, of not having this work performed?

Quantify Your Work

All consultants should keep in mind that numbers are the language of business. Everything is measurable. Include a measurement component for all your work so that you can demonstrate that you have produced results. For every project you conduct, quantify your client's status quo before, during, and after your work. Use multiple types of measures. Be creative in what you measure and how you measure it, but make certain that you are measuring important outcomes. For example:

- An organizational development consultant can measure improvements in employee morale, satisfaction, and turnover and translate this into dollars.

- A marketing consultant can measure improvements in customer awareness, understanding, and sales.

- A training consultant can measure how his or her training improved productivity.

- An executive coaching consultant can measure the views of an employee's manager, peers, subordinates, and customers before and after the coaching and determine how the improvement has led to improved work flow and reduced time spent on projects.

Demonstrating results is critically important. If you are offering a service where the results of your work are so intangible they cannot be measured, you should seriously consider offering a different type of service.

Conclusion

Producing tangible results is one of the most important things you can do to keep your gas tank filled. If you are able to consistently produce positive quantifiable results, you will likely enjoy a continuing flow of new business.

CHAPTER 15

Make Certain Your Recommendations Are Implemented

A FEW YEARS AGO a friend of mine, Wellesley, Massachusetts-based management psychologist and executive coach Paul Powers, was consulting to Sports Plus, a 200-employee, $20 million New England sporting goods manufacturer. Paul served as the consigliere to John, the founder and CEO of the company, as well as management trainer for John's four direct reports.

John was very much an employee-oriented employer. He knew all his employees well and treated them like family. He worked hard, often six and a half days per week, paid his employees well, and made certain they received all the support they needed.

John was approaching retirement age and wanted to eventually turn the business over to his son Jack. Jack had worked summers at the company while he attended college. He knew a great deal about administration, human resources, receiving, and manufacturing but had never held any position of major responsibilities. Now that he had graduated, Jack wanted to work in a senior management position.

Paul advised John to have his son work elsewhere first so that he could gain some experience and feel successful. That way the son would be able to bring more to the company when he eventually joined it and would be confident that he could succeed on his own without having anything delivered to him on a sliver platter.

John found his son a job through a fellow Rotary Club member who was chairman of another manufacturer in the area. The chairman had hired a nonfamily CEO to run the company, and he hired Jack to work as the COO beneath him.

A few years later, the chairman contacted John and said it was time for him to take his son back. Apparently, it wasn't working out well for Jack. Although he was a competent manager of business operations, he didn't get along well with his boss, the CEO. He also was not treating employees with respect.

John rationalized that Jack was meant to lead, not follow the direction of someone else. So he decided to step back and become chairman of his own company and bring Jack in as the president.

Paul advised against this because he had not been genuinely successful at the other company. But John insisted. He was receiving pressure from his wife to travel and spend less time at the company.

Under Jack's reign, the company began to decline and just three years later was forced to sell to a European company. Paul had seen it coming, but John had not taken his advice. In retrospect, Paul thinks he should have taken his concerns to the board of directors. His real client was Sports Plus, not John.

The Challenge

Unfortunately, this is an all too common occurrence for consultants. You spend several months or even years getting to understand your clients, the difficulties they are experiencing, and what can be done to improve their situation. You then offer a series of carefully crafted recommendations. What happens next? *Nothing.* The client disregards your recommendations, and your report just sits on a dusty shelf.

You collect your fee, check in periodically to see if they have implemented your recommendations, and become disappointed when your calls and e-mails aren't returned. Although you stand by your recommendations and sincerely believe they will improve your client's condition, you feel like you didn't really accomplish anything of value. Also, you worry that you will probably not receive any repeat business or glowing referrals from the client.

It's like a pass from a quarterback to a receiver. No matter how well the ball is thrown, it's just not a good pass if the receiver doesn't catch it. Your recommendations are worthless unless your client uses them.

Your credibility as a consultant and your ability to land repeat business will most likely depend upon the successful use of your recommendations and the tangible results they yield. Without these results, your gas tank of new business will eventually be empty.

Solutions

Some methods follow for increasing the probability that your recommendations are implemented.

Discuss Implementation Issues Even Before Starting the Project

At the initial meeting with your client, discuss in detail the process they will use to implement your recommendations. Be sure to ask these types of questions:

- When the study has been completed, what's the best way to make certain that my recommendations will be implemented?
- With other successful projects conducted here, what was the best process for making certain the results were used?
- Who will receive the recommendations?
- Who will own the responsibility for implementing the recommendations?
- What role will senior management play?
- What is the time frame for implementation?

Include an agreed-upon implementation process as part of your proposal. Make it clear to your prospect that success will depend on implementation. Emphasize that your relationship with them will be a partnership and that both parties have obligations to meet. At a minimum, include in your project plan an initial step in which the implementation process will be mapped out, documented, and communicated to the appropriate parties.

Involve the Client in Developing the Recommendations

You've heard plenty of lawyer jokes, I'm sure. One of the more well-known consultant jokes is "If you ask a consultant what time of day it is, they will ask to borrow your watch, tell you the time, and then keep the watch." There is some truth to this. Just as therapists involve their patients in developing solutions to their personal problems, good consultants involve their clients in developing solutions to their organizational problems.

Avoid "hit-and-run consulting," in which you conduct the work, provide your recommendations, and then leave. With this approach, the odds that the client's condition will improve are very low.

Conceptually, all consulting engagements involve a continuous cycling of three processes:

◻ **Entry:** The consultant enters the organization by developing a written contract about the work that will be performed and how it will benefit the organization.

◻ **Data Gathering:** The consultant then gathers data for the client through interviews, observations, or analysis of data.

◻ **Feedback:** The consultant then delivers the data and conclusions back to clients in a way that they can understand and use.

◻ **Repeat the Cycle:** The consultant then develops an agreement with the client about using the data that has been gathered, gathering more data, and feeding it back to the client again. This three-step process continues until the condition of the client has improved and the relationship is terminated.

It is important for you to organize your engagement with the client as an ongoing process in which you gather information, provide information to them, assess their reactions, and move them forward toward implementing positive actions. Include steps in your process such as:

◻ **A preliminary feedback meeting:** In this session, you share your preliminary observations with the client, test some of your hypotheses, and ask what they believe the implications of your findings are. This will help you to fine-tune your recommendations so that they are more digestible for your client.

◻ **A feedback/brainstorming session:** Plan to ask your client for ideas on how the organization will use the information you have given them. Then partner with them to formulate recommendations.

◻ **A post-feedback meeting:** Plan to meet with your client after you have presented your recommendations. During this session, discuss the client's interpretations of your findings and the preliminary plans for using it.

Understand What Is Realistic and Practical

Make certain to meet with the appropriate people, ask the appropriate questions, and dig as deeply as possible. You need to understand the organization's culture before you can make realistic recommendations. For example, if you are working with an organization that is strapped for cash, recommendations requiring significant sums of money will not be implemented.

Try to meet with all the key players, agree on how to define the problem, ask how they have tried to solve the problem in the past, and discuss what they think might work now.

Make Certain You Meet with the Key Decision-Makers

Sometimes clients will intentionally refuse to give you access to the key executives. They might be fearful of relinquishing control, not want to be one-upped by you, or prefer the opportunity to present the results themselves to the decision-makers. Unfortunately, without this access, the odds that your recommendations will be implemented are low.

Outline for your clients why it is in their best interest to provide you with access to key decision-makers. If this fails, offer to visit executives along with them to gather data and to jointly present results and recommendations.

Provide a Range of Options

Your clients will have an easier time relating to your recommendations if you provide a broad range of options rather than a single solution. Each option should be supported by your data and findings. For each recommendation, cite the findings that led to the recommendation, and then provide several options for how they can be implemented. Present your list of recommendations in order of priority.

Become Part of the Implementation Team

Make assisting in the implementation of your recommendations part of the overall project. If possible, fold this in to your project fee rather than showing it as a separate line item to prevent your client from eliminating this critical step. Make clients understand that involving you in the implementation process is a good way for them to protect their investment.

Follow Up to Monitor Progress

Offer to meet with your client, perhaps gratis, to help implement your recommendations. Show clients that you really care about their success. Offer to visit them at any time to discuss how they can move forward.

Conclusion

Don't be a hit-and-run consultant who presents recommendations and then moves on to the next client. Always keep in mind that you will only be successful as a consultant if your clients achieve the results they are seeking.

CHAPTER 16

Maximizing the Value of Networking Meetings

HAVE BEEN A LOYAL MEMBER of the Society of Professional Consultants (SPC: www.spconsultants.org) for many years. SPC is a regional professional association, based in Massachusetts, dedicated to supporting independent consultants through education, mentoring, and networking. At one meeting several years ago, I met Mike Greystone, who had spent thirty years as a human resource professional for several large manufacturers. He had recently left his job to start a management training consulting practice. His business was struggling, and he was beginning to question whether he should continue or look for another full-time job.

I tried to help Mike by giving him advice and providing emotional support. We became good friends. His business eventually righted itself, and he has been an independent consultant now for more than ten years.

One day he mentioned to me that he was consulting to his former company, a 25,000-employee global manufacturer, and that they were looking for a firm to help them conduct an employee survey. He said that he had recommended me, and he gave me the name of the person to call. One thing led to another, and they became a six-figure client of mine.

How did this happen? It wasn't because I attended SPC meetings with a goal of promoting my services. It was because I went to each meeting with the mindset of trying to help others. Mike didn't feel he owed me this referral. But because I helped him and he trusted me, he was happy to refer me to his client.

The Challenge

Many people dislike attending professional networking meetings. They feel they are expensive and a waste of time. They also dread having to make small talk and be social. However, as shown in the Table 16-1, this is what successful consultants do.

TABLE 16-1. ATTENDANCE AT PROFESSIONAL MEETINGS BY THE CONSULTING 200.

What type of marketing activities do you conduct on a consistent basis?	
Professional meetings attended by my prospects	64%
Professional meetings attended by those in my field	57%
Professional meetings attended primarily by other consultants	36%

As previously mentioned, 82 percent of The Consulting 200 say that the majority of their business comes from word-of-mouth referrals. The more mouths you listen to, the higher the probability that you will receive referrals.

Solutions

Here are eight ways to maximize the value of professional networking meetings.

Be Strategic About Which Meetings You Attend

Networking in the wrong places won't help you or your business. I suggest that three different types of professional networking groups have the most value:

1. **Professional development groups:** Join a group that will enable you to keep abreast of the latest developments in your field. For

example, if you are a marketing professional, you should be attending meetings such as the American Marketing Association to keep up with the latest advances in the field. If you are a chemical engineer, you should join an association of chemical engineers.

2. **Groups of other consultants:** Join a group of consultants, such as the Institute of Management Consultants (www.imcusa.org), that will enable you to learn more about marketing, sales, and client relations. Fellow consultants are also a great source for support and referrals.

3. **Join a group that will allow you to interact with your prospects:** If you sell to CFOs, then you should attend the meetings they attend. If you sell to executive directors of nonprofit organizations, you should attend the meetings they attend.

Join Associations Where You Are Able to Interact with Others

I used to belong to a human resource association that held breakfast meetings. Unfortunately, the people I wanted to meet would show up just minutes before the speaker began and would dart out as soon as the speaker ended. There was also only one small operating committee, with little opportunity for participation.

When deciding which networking groups to join, consider how much time is actually available to network. Some professional groups have very few, if any, committees and allow hardly any time for networking. Avoid these meetings.

Become an Active Member

It is much better to be active in one professional association than to periodically attend meetings of five or ten. Once you become active, people in the association get to know who you are and what you do. It takes time for people to recognize you, view you as a colleague rather than a stranger, and trust you enough to recommend you to others.

Volunteer to serve on a committee or the board of directors. Try to get involved in activities that will enable you to interact with others. For example, it makes much more sense to join the membership committee than to volunteer to go off on your own and rewrite the association's bylaws. Get to know the movers and shakers. Each association has a few key people who know everybody else and can make things happen.

Attend Meetings with the Right Mindset

You can spot naive networkers from across the room. They come to networking meetings with a desperate mindset: "How can I get referrals and new business?" They spend the meeting darting from one conversation to another, furiously passing out their business cards and saying things like, "Let me know if you hear of anyone who needs my services" and "Call me if you hear of anything." This approach not only doesn't work, it is a big turnoff to others.

Instead, it is better to come to networking meetings with the mindset: "How can I help others at the meeting?" or "I would like to meet at least one person tonight who I can meet with one-on-one at a later time," or "I am really curious about what others at this meeting do for a living."

There are many ways you can help others. You can, for example:

- Provide introductions.
- Recommend books or websites.
- Provide information about people, companies, or trends.
- Simply listen and offer emotional support.

Try to sit with people who you don't know and focus on how you can help them. Try to introduce people who you think can provide value to each other. Offer to swap business cards if there is a good reason to keep in touch.

Ask Questions

Instead of worrying about what you will say to others about yourself and your business, focus instead on asking questions. There is no greater compliment you can bestow on someone than to ask them about themselves. Simple open-ended questions are best, such as, "Tell me what you do for a living," or "What challenges is your business facing these days?" This can be a great way to start and maintain meaningful conversations. Come to the meeting with an inquisitive attitude.

Come Early and Stay Late

Inexperienced networkers come to meetings late and leave as soon as the speaker has finished. The best opportunities for networking are usually before the start of the formal program and immediately afterwards. If you come only to listen to the speaker, you are missing out on much of the value the meeting can provide.

Follow Up Immediately

Does this ever happen to you? You meet someone at a professional meeting, exchange business cards, suggest that you follow up with each other, and then nothing happens. You go back to your office and put the card near the phone but never make the call. Two weeks later you look at the card and say to yourself, "Who is that person?"

It is important to follow up immediately, while the person and the conversation are fresh in both your minds. Write notes to yourself on the person's business card. E-mail the person immediately after the meeting or the following day. The e-mail might be to ask a question, provide some information, set up a possible lunch meeting, or just to say you enjoyed the conversation. Use the subject line "Following up."

Don't Try to Sell

Selling at professional meetings is usually inappropriate. Instead, use the meeting as an opportunity to develop a relationship and then schedule a meeting for a later date. If you meet a prospect at a meeting, suggest a time for you to get together, or e-mail them the next day. You might also send them information about your work that you believe they would find valuable.

Conclusion

As a consultant, your professional network is one of your most valuable assets. Professional networking meetings are one of the best ways to revitalize and grow your network. But if you attend meetings without a clear strategy for maximizing their value, you may end up as a wallflower, merely watching other people network and wondering why you gave up the time in the first place.

CHAPTER 17

Marketing Even When You're Busy

Gary Patterson of Fiscal Doctor (www.fiscaldoctor.com) provides strategic consulting and risk management surveys across the country. He helps CEOs, board members, executive teams, and private equity investors and owners achieve financial health. He travels the country, often spending several weeks or months at a client's site. This makes it challenging for him to market on a continuous basis.

Gary tries very hard in both good times and bad to set aside one day per week for marketing and meeting people. He also goes out of his way to help people who are in career transition. He says, "It is a nice thing to do, but I also know that when they eventually land in a new position, these people will remember those who have helped them." Gary also tries to stay in touch regularly with his network by sending out brief e-mails containing valuable information.

Sarah Johnson is a senior human resource management consultant. For many years she has served as an interim vice president of human resources for organizations that are in need of a temporary department head while they search for a new VP to fill the position.

There have been many times when Sarah has been able to transition smoothly from one assignment to another, but often there are large periods of time when she has no clients and needs to aggressively market to find her next one.

Over the years, Sarah has learned that even when she is busy she still must:

◻ Attend the monthly professional association meetings of the several human resource organizations to which she belongs.

◻ Keep in telephone contact with the core members of her professional network.

◻ Continue to write her monthly e-newsletter.

◻ Keep her website up-to-date.

The Challenge

Marketing is a challenge for both beginning consultants and experienced consultants busy with client work. To keep a consulting practice thriving and to avoid the agonizing cycles of feast and famine, it is critically important that you never stop marketing. When the marketing stops, the all-important lead stream dries up. Once this happens, it won't be long before you will be in a panic, desperately trying to find new business.

Solutions

Some ways to keep marketing even when you are busy follow.

Figure Out What Type of Marketing You Enjoy

As previously mentioned, most marketing strategies are effective when done properly and often enough. The "often enough" part is crucial. If you don't enjoy it, you probably won't do it. It's as simple as that. For many consultants, marketing activities such as cold calling, speaking, getting published, and attending networking meetings never get off the back burner. Why? Because they hate doing them.

Some consultants love to write, while others have difficulty putting a coherent sentence together. Some love to schmooze at professional meetings, while others would rather stay home and read a good book. Some love to deliver speeches, while others would prefer to have bamboo shoved up their fingernails than get up in front of a group.

You need to determine which methods of marketing you enjoy the most. If you enjoy it, you'll do it, even when you're busy with client work.

If you enjoy getting up in front of groups, then look for as many speaking opportunities as possible. Particularly if you are willing to speak for free, it is quite easy to find groups that are looking for speakers. Just contact the association's president or program chair and tell them about the topics that you can present that would be valuable to their members.

If you prefer to meet with people one-on-one, then look for as many networking opportunities as possible. Breakfast, lunch, dinner, coffee, or drinks provide opportunities to meet with people. Several of my colleagues have confided that they can tell how good a job they are doing at networking just by looking at the bathroom scale. When they are frequently meeting people for meals, they start to gain weight.

If you enjoy writing, then start an electronic newsletter and launch new issues on a strict schedule. Send it to everyone you know, both in your business and personal lives. Ask people to forward it to others.

Conduct Regularly Scheduled Marketing Activities

Left to chance, even marketing activities you enjoy will remain stuck on the back burner if you don't schedule them. Block out time or schedule due dates for your marketing activities. Tasks that are placed on your calendar are more likely to be completed. Schedule items that you can control, such as completing a paper, sending out direct mail pieces, or attending monthly professional meetings.

If you are a member of a professional association, attend every meeting. Mark the dates for the entire year on your calendar and make attendance a priority.

Leverage the Content in Your Marketing

Developing new intellectual content is time-consuming. Recycle your own intellectual property so that you won't have to reinvent the wheel every time you turn your attention toward marketing. For example, if you write a paper for a professional publication, you can use that content in speeches, in your newsletter, in direct mail pieces, on your website, and in press releases.

Develop a Realistic Marketing Schedule and Stick to It

Develop a marketing plan each year that lists the monthly marketing activities you are going to conduct. For example, list articles you are going to write, mailings you are going to conduct, cold calls you are going to make, and advertisements you are going to place.

Make certain that your plan is realistic. The most important part of making a plan is sticking to it. Place due dates on your calendar so that you can schedule your client work around them even when you're busy.

Be certain that your marketing objectives are S.M.A.R.T:

- **Specific:** You might establish a marketing objective of conducting one networking meeting per week, but to make it a more specific objective, identify which four people you will meet with that month.

- **Measurable:** You should be able to look back at your marketing objectives and know quantitatively whether you achieved them.

- **Attainable:** If your marketing objectives are unattainable, you probably won't even attempt to achieve them. For example, instead of completing a book by the end of the week, completing a book chapter might be more attainable. Set objectives that are challenging but possible.

- **Realistic:** Don't commit to doing more marketing than you believe is actually possible. You must be willing and able to accomplish the objective, and you must believe it can be accomplished. Be certain, however, that each specific objective represents substantial progress.

◘ **Timely:** You need to set fixed due dates for your marketing objectives. Without a sense of urgency, you will not attain your goals.

Make Your Website Work for You 24/7

A website can perform some of your marketing for you on a continuous basis, even while you sleep. You can use your website to:

◘ Sign up new subscribers to your newsletter.

◘ Enable visitors to download free reports.

◘ Conduct a survey and provide respondents with results.

◘ Sell products such as books, CDs, DVDs, and papers.

◘ Advertise your services.

It is important that you update your website regularly with new content. If you are not technically savvy, hire a good Webmaster to help you.

Be Careful with Your Time

Some of the business models described in Part I allow you to have more control of your time. For example, if you are selling your time rather than charging for projects or products, you may not be able to devote the time and attention you need toward marketing your services.

Also, be careful about spending a lot of time traveling. Travel eats up valuable time and energy. Try to arrange some of your client meetings via telephone or through Web conferencing services.

Delegate Marketing Activities

If you sincerely believe that using consultants is good for your clients, why isn't it good for you? They can help you strategize and develop an effective, realistic marketing plan. There are many who work with small businesses just like yours.

Once you have developed a plan, you can use others to help you implement it. There is no reason that you need to do all of your own website development, brochure development, cold calling, or any other marketing activity.

Conclusion

Marketing is the most important part of your consulting business. Make it part of your routine, both when you are busy and when you are not. Follow the strategies above to avoid experiencing only peaks and valleys.

PART 4

Avoiding Road Hazards

CHAPTER 18

Losing Your Motivation

FOR THE PAST TEN YEARS, business had been very good for
Harvey Wigder's executive search and compensation firm (www.
fulcrumgroup.com). It seemed like new business just came to him
without having to do much marketing. He had established a niche for
placing senior executives in small, privately held businesses and was
feeling good about what he had accomplished.

But then the economic recession hit, and business slowed dramatically. He realized that he had become complacent. He had gradually stopped doing many of the things that had made his business a
success, such as regularly attending professional meetings, writing
an electronic newsletter, and keeping in contact with former clients.
He needed to remotivate himself.

Harvey had been an independent consultant for more than thirty
years and had experienced similar drops in business during other
times in his career. Each time he was able to dig deep inside and
re-energize himself.

This time, he committed himself to focusing his business solely on executive search, relaunching his website, writing his newsletter more regularly, initiating a direct mail campaign, finishing the book he had started, meeting more frequently with his network of former clients, joining more professional associations, and attending meetings more frequently.

More commonly, consultants lose their motivation when their business slows, and they have a difficult time re-energizing themselves. Some lose their motivation even when business is good because they become bored. Losing one's motivation can be a major road hazard on the journey to a successful consulting business.

The Challenge

A high level of energy and enthusiasm is critically important for consultants. Without it they will be unable to:

- Continually provide high-quality service to clients.
- Consistently market their services.
- Handle rejection from prospects.
- Keep the faith during periods when business is slow.

Solutions

Several ways to maintain a high level of motivation in your consulting practice follow.

Relish Your Independence

As a consultant, you own your time and space. No more clock watching, fighting traffic during your daily commutes, playing office politics, or worrying about losing your job due to a merger or downsizing. Enjoy your freedom! You've taken great risks to earn your emancipation. Don't take it for granted. Ask yourself if you are committed enough to maintain the professional lifestyle you have created. You probably are.

Remind Yourself of the Value of Your Work

What you do for your clients is important. If it weren't, none of them would pay you to do it. Clients don't pay just to be nice. They have paid you in the past and will continue to do so because you fill an important need for them. You are providing value by helping them make money, save money, or somehow improve their organization.

If you feel you are losing your energy, reread your marketing literature and some of the articles you have written. If you still believe in what you have been preaching, which you probably do, this will re-energize you.

Create a Mission Statement

Big companies have them, and so should you. A well-written mission statement defines your organization for both you and your clients. It outlines how you will provide value to your clients and to the business community. It creates a philosophical anchor for all of your activities, including marketing and client work.

A carefully crafted mission statement that captures how you are providing value to your clients can help regenerate your enthusiasm.

Sit down one day and take a crack at writing your mission statement. Make it something that you can relate to and that succinctly captures the essence of your business. Have others review it for you before you finalize it. Then post it on your wall, carry it around with you, include it in your proposals, and incorporate it into your elevator speech when you meet new people.

Continue to Grow

Doing the same work in the same way over and over again can become boring. As a consultant, you have the flexibility to take additional training and to begin offering new services. Pushing yourself to expand your horizons can be challenging—and therefore energizing.

Do More of What You Enjoy

Your marketing efforts will be more effective if you focus on the tasks that you enjoy and so too will your consulting practice. If you like to write, sell your writing services. If you like to speak, hire a speaker's agent. If you like to work on a particular type of consulting assignment, focus your marketing efforts on obtaining more of that type of work.

Remind Yourself Why You Started Your Business

Did you become a consultant in order to avoid a full-time job, gain more flexibility in your life, or do more of the kinds of work you really enjoy? These reasons are probably still valid for you today.

Conclusion

Consulting can be the greatest way in the world to make a living. If you feel your energy start to wane, step back and take stock of all the advantages in the life of a consultant versus the alternative of working for an organization. If you can recommit yourself, you will regain the energy and enthusiasm you need to prosper.

CHAPTER 19

Becoming Lonely

OFTEN CONDUCT outplacement workshops for employees who were recently laid off from their jobs. During these two-day sessions I discuss topics such as preparing a good resume, answering difficult interview questions, networking your way to a job, and negotiating.

During the first morning of the workshop, we discuss how to handle the emotional loss of losing a job. I begin by writing on a flip chart the question, "What are you going to have to replace?" The first responses are invariably "the salary" and "the benefits." I then ask what else they are going to have to replace. In almost every workshop I conduct, the next word that comes from the group is "friends."

Consciously or unconsciously, most people derive a great deal of pleasure in the workplace from the social stimulation they receive from others. Being around others, talking at the watercooler, eating lunch with coworkers, attending meetings with others, working on teams, and discussing work and other matters with colleagues are very important to most workers.

Working with others helps employees to develop a shared understanding of what is often a stressful situation. Because others constantly validate the quality of their work, it allows them to feel good about themselves. It helps them to feel part of something bigger than themselves (e.g., a cause or a mission, even if that cause is simply to make the business a success). Coworkers also provide emotional support and comfort.

The Challenge

One of the prices many independent consultants pay for their freedom and independence is the loss of this type of daily social stimulation. For some, this is not an important consequence. But for many, loneliness and lack of interaction with others can be very difficult.

I'll admit it. I am one of those people who gets lonely. Although I cherish my independence, I am a social person. Working in my home office every day can be lonely, especially during weeks when I have very few appointments. I look forward to the end of the day when my wife comes home from her school psychologist job at a local high school. After working a full day with people all around her and constant social stimulation, however, she often prefers, at least for a few hours, to be left alone. Oh, well!

Survey Results: Independent Consulting Can Be Lonely.

About one-third of The Consulting 200 say they are often lonely being an independent consultant.

I often find that working as an independent consultant is lonely.

Percent	
33	Strongly agree or agree
29	Partly agree/Partly disagree
38	Disagree or strongly disagree

Solutions

A few suggestions follow for fighting the loneliness of the life of an independent consultant.

Rent Office Space

Dan King, founder and owner of Career Planning and Management, Inc. (www.careerfirm.com), works out of a rented office in a small, historic three-story office building in downtown Boston. Over the years he has made good friends with the people who operate businesses in the other small offices within the building. They have become his "watercooler buddies."

Work Out of an Office-Sharing Center

Fellow outplacement instructor Lisa Kirby Gibbs (www.Highland-March.com) owns and operates a shared office center. Her tenants are mostly small businesses that share conference and training rooms, a reception area, and the administrative services her staff provides. The people from each of the different businesses have gotten to know each other well over the years and have become good friends. They actively network with one another and share referrals.

Create a Support Group

Take a lesson from the many stay-at-home moms and dads who join playgroups. The real reason they get together with other parents is to chat and share the challenges, frustrations, and joys of child rearing. Create a support group of fellow consultants and meet regularly to share what's going well and what's not going so well with your businesses.

One group I met with for many years, the Enterprise Group, consisted of six senior consultants. Every two weeks we met for dinner at one of our homes. We took turns hosting and making or ordering the dinner. In addition to sharing thoughts about our personal lives and businesses, we also joined forces to plan and host quarterly networking breakfast meetings for our combined network of contacts.

Another group I have met with on a monthly basis for many

years is called the BreakFitz group. Five consultants meet each month at a local hotel for breakfast and to share our business successes and challenges.

Attend Professional Meetings with Other Consultants

Over the years, I have found interacting with fellow consultants at professional meetings, such as the Society of Professional Consultants and the Institute of Management Consultants, to be quite comforting. Attendees at these meetings share a special affinity. We are all trying to make a living from our small consulting businesses. We share a common bond and kinship. Some of my closest friends are fellow consultants I have met through these organizations.

Meet with Colleagues on a Regular Basis

It is important to get out of your office. Schedule at least one breakfast, lunch, or dinner meeting with a colleague, prospect, or client each week. In addition to sharing ideas and learning about what is happening outside your little office, you will be less lonely.

Reach Out via Telephone

If you are working alone out of your office all day, make it a habit to pick up the phone and call someone every few hours. You don't have to have a specific reason to call a friend, family member, or colleague. Just call to check in and say hello.

Plan Something Social Every Day

Get out of your office and interact with others as often as you can. If you are alone all day every day, you need to push yourself to interact with others. Have lunch with a colleague, go to the gym, or meet a friend for coffee.

Plan Something Fun Every Day

Tennis, poker, yoga, playing the piano, watching a ball game, or doing any other extracurricular activity that you enjoy will suffice. You need to have something other than your work to look forward to every day.

Conclusion

Loneliness can be a major road hazard for independent consultants. The life of an independent consultant can be all-consuming, especially if you work from your home. Although most consultants value their freedom from a corporate environment, many feel they are never able to totally escape their work.

You need to be proactive and develop strategies for frequently interacting with others. Create your own watercooler.

CHAPTER 20

Diluting Your Business Model

FIRST STARTED CONSULTING while teaching at a small liberal arts college. I established ongoing subcontracting relationships with several small consulting firms. For one firm, I wrote training manuals to teach managers how to conduct performance appraisals. For another, I conducted focus groups with industry experts to help companies identify new products to manufacture. And for another, I developed selection tests to help them hire people who would stay with the company long term.

Eventually, I was earning much more money from consulting than teaching. After a few years I stopped teaching and pursued my subcontracting activities full time. I continued to build my fledgling consulting practice by conducting direct mail campaigns to local consulting firms, offering my services as a subcontractor.

Business was good. I was almost 100 percent billable. I had seven consulting firm "clients" and felt I had found a nice niche. When business was slow with one firm, there were always a few others I could count on to send work my way.

After a while, however, I realized that my business model had several flaws. First, there was a limit to how much I could charge. What made me attractive to these consulting firms was that they could mark up my fees two to three times and make a hefty profit.

A second problem was that I had no specific clients who I could rely on for referrals or testimonials. The clients belonged to the consulting firms I was subcontracting to, not me. I couldn't even legitimately place them on a client list. My relationships with the clients were inconsequential.

A third problem was that I wasn't performing or learning the skills I would need in order to land my own clients. For example, I wasn't marketing directly to clients, I wasn't writing proposals, and I wasn't pricing my services. I needed to become more skilled in these areas in order to grow my business and increase my income.

After about three years of operating my business this way, I accepted a job at a large international consulting firm, with the goal of learning how to land my own "real" clients. When I left that firm four years later to start my own consulting practice, I vowed to limit how much, if any, subcontracting work I would perform. I did not want to dilute my business model.

Here is another example of how your business model can become diluted. At another stage of my consulting career, in addition to my consulting work I frequently partnered with a consulting firm in a nearby state that provided a broad range of human resource consulting services. I served as their employee survey guru. They referred employee survey business to me, but I needed to work under their auspices. They gave me business cards with their firm's name on it, and I became an extension of their firm. We developed a formula for sharing the revenue and expenses. I conducted all the work but made less money then I would have if I had found the client myself. I was willing to do this because it didn't conflict with my other work, and it brought me work that I would not otherwise have found.

Eventually, as our relationship grew, I began helping them market our services. I gave speeches and conducted mailings under their firm's name. When I landed a new client, we divided the revenue, but

I did almost all the work. I gradually realized that I was not making as much money as I should for both landing the client and fulfilling the contract. Eventually, we amicably parted ways.

The Challenge

Some money is better than no money, especially when business is slow. That's why it is often tempting to bypass your preferred business model by subcontracting, partnering, or engaging in other moneymaking activities. The problem is that this dilutes your business. It detracts from your identity in the marketplace, it limits the time available for you to market your services, and it usually reduces your long-term income potential.

Solutions

Limit or Avoid Subcontracting

Be very careful about committing your valuable time to subcontracting for other consulting firms. It will limit your ability to pursue work that is more consistent with your firm's mission.

There are exceptions of course. You might consider subcontracting if:

- The subcontracting work is totally different from the primary work you provide to your target market. If, for example, you provide executive coaching services, it would not adversely affect your image in the marketplace if you accepted a subcontracting position to conduct focus groups.

- The subcontracting work is countercyclical to your business. I have a subcontracting relationship with a firm for which I conduct outplacement workshops. Typically, the outplacement business is booming at the same time that my employee survey business is in less demand, and vice versa. It is important, however, that I don't stop marketing my employee survey business while I am conducting outplacement workshops.

- The subcontracting work will help you develop professionally. Some subcontracting will provide you with valuable experience and knowledge that will eventually help you to expand your own business. If this is the case, it may well make good business sense for you to subcontract.

Limit or Avoid Partnering

Partnering can also dilute your business. It can lead you astray from making it on your own as a self-sufficient consultant. It can also reduce your potential earnings, since you will have to support the financial needs of your partner(s) as well as yourself.

When considering partnering with others, the most important question to ask is "Will one plus one equal three?" In other words, will having a partner provide you with significantly more business than you would have on your own?

Here are some of the wrong reasons to partner.

I don't like marketing or sales so I'll let my partner handle that end of things. Some would disagree, but I believe that in order to succeed as an independent consultant you will have to learn how to market and sell your services effectively. No one can represent your knowledge and experience better than you.

I need the emotional support a partner can provide. Emotional support is important but you don't need to share your revenue with someone else to get it.

Here are some reasons why partnering might make sense:

You will be able to provide significantly greater value to your clients. If you and your partner can provide much greater value to your client than you would be able to provide alone, it might make sense to take on a partner. It is important, however, that your client see the value as well and be willing to pay more than the combined total of what you would receive separately.

You will be able to learn a great deal from a partner, which you will eventually use on your own. If your long-term plan is to extricate yourself from the partnership, then it might make sense for you to enter into the arrangement so that you can help yourself in the long run. But be honest with your partner about your intentions.

Partnering would expose you to a market to which you otherwise would have little or no access. If your partner has an established name and reputation in a particular niche, it might make sense for you to join forces.

Be Clear on Your Business Model and Be Cautious About Deviating from It

You need to maintain a strategic outlook about your business. Straying from your business model can be a prescription for failure. Before switching models from a project-based or retainer-based business to a subcontracting or strategic relationship model, think about whether you need to market differently, focus more on a particular niche, or change the type of services you are providing.

Conclusion

Diluting your business model is another of the many hazards on the road to building and maintaining a successful consultancy. At some point in your career you might want to reinvent yourself, but this has to be a focused, strategic decision. Haphazardly straying from your business model can create huge potholes that absorb your precious time and energy.

CHAPTER 21

Charging Too Little

R OY JOHNSON, A DENTIST, is a friend and client. He has owned
and operated a small dental practice in southern New Jersey for the
past thirty years. He provides a variety of state-of-the-art services,
including preventive, restorative, and cosmetic dentistry, and treatment of bite disorders. He shared with me that he was having a problem with dental insurance companies, which had become unwilling
to reimburse him at a level where he could profitably provide his full
range of high-level services.

Roy made a strategic business decision. He decided to no longer
accept dental insurance payments for his services. He knew that if he
continued to accept the low level of reimbursement from the insurance companies, he would need to change his business model to a
fast-paced, production-oriented business. He was unwilling to do
this, as it would involve:

◻ Employing at least one person to handle the insurance paperwork
◻ Limiting the time he could spend with patients

◻   Compromising the quality of the materials he could use

Roy felt that these changes would greatly diminish the value he was providing to patients. It was not the way he wanted to conduct his business. More importantly to him, accepting insurance meant that he would need to serve many patients who didn't fit his ideal profile (i.e., people who really care about their oral health and are willing to pay in order to receive the best care and treatment possible).

The great risk, of course, was that it would be more difficult to find patients who valued his services enough that they were willing to pay his fees out of their own pockets. But his practice is located in a relatively wealthy part of the state, and he felt that not accepting insurance was a risk he was willing to take. He was confident that there were patients who would be willing to spend their discretionary income on his health-related services.

The patient satisfaction survey I conducted for him showed that his patients really did value the quality of the care they received. That gave him the confidence to make this shift. It was a decision based on both the economics of the situation and his passion for providing a high level of service to health-conscious patients.

Roy now has to spend more time marketing and promoting his services than he would like. The challenge he must overcome is that many people don't really understand the many differences between average and high-quality dentistry. But he has survived, and he is confident that his business will thrive because he is offering more value than he could possibly offer under an insurance-driven model that supports mediocrity rather than quality. He is providing the type of care he wants to provide to patients who value it. He and his team are happier, and his patients value their high level of care.

The Challenge

The balance between mass-market and average quality on the one hand and filling a smaller niche with a high-quality product or service on the other is a challenge faced by many consultants. It is also a major road hazard on the way to developing a successful consulting business. There are always people who are willing to offer similar services for less money. The competition can come from less experienced consultants, Web-based services, or consultants based in less expensive parts of the world.

In the face of this competition, it is very tempting to lower your prices in order to land new business. However, unless you are willing and able to make up the lost revenue in volume, lowering your prices may be your business's death knell.

Here are six reasons why you should avoid lowering your prices:

1. **Your goal is to make enough money to support you and your family.** As discussed in chapter 2, you need to be able to charge enough money that you can pay your business expenses, fund your health and retirement benefits, and pay yourself the salary you need.

2. **Lowering your fees won't necessarily lead to more business.** Lowering your fees can backfire by cheapening the value of your services. In the long run, it is usually better to be known as the high-quality, higher-cost provider than the lower-cost, lower-quality provider. Undoubtedly, there will always be someone who can underbid you. Avoid this type of contest.

3. **There is no such thing as a one-time lower price.** Some consultants believe that they can offer a low price to get their foot in the door with a client and then eventually raise their prices once the client gains respect for their work. This is rarely the case. If anything, your clients will want to pay you less for future business.

4. **You will need to compromise the value of your services.** Lowering your fees may require you to offer services that are less useful to your clients. This may limit your opportunity for repeat business from that client or for their testimonials and referrals.

5. **You will attract clients that don't fit your ideal profile.** Lowering your prices may make you less, rather than more, attractive to the very clients that you are seeking. Most people know that they get what they pay for. If you cost less, they will perceive you as being worth less.

6. **If it comes down to cost, then you've already lost.** If your prospects don't see that you offer significantly more value than those who are charging a rock-bottom price, you will have little chance to win the competition.

Solutions

Charging too little is a surefire way of failing as an independent consultant. Use the following strategies to help you avoid undercharging.

Target the Right Prospects

Find prospects who are likely to value what you offer and are willing to pay for that value. For example, if you provide sophisticated, high-end Web design, it doesn't make sense for you to market your services to one-person businesses.

Find Ways to Deliver More Value

If you find that you are constantly competing against firms that provide services at a lower cost than you can provide, instead of lowering your costs, find ways to increase the value you provide. For example, if you offer speaking coaching services to senior executives, offer value-added services, such as videotaping their speeches or attending their speeches to provide them with on-the-spot, live feedback.

Get Your Prospects to Articulate the Value You Provide

If a prospect says that there are other firms that can provide similar work for less cost, rather than spouting off about how you provide more value than your competitors, try asking, "What value do you believe I can provide that others cannot?" They may say, "None," but it is more likely that they will have a specific answer for you. If so, it will help you close the sale more effectively than if you were to tell them why *you* think you offer more value.

Offer Options

As mentioned in chapter 13, it is important to provide your prospects with options, each with a different price. Offer at least three, each with various levels of service. Although they may select the low-cost option, at least you won't be providing the highest level of service for that fee.

Be Prepared to Walk Away

One of the most important principles of negotiating is the willingness to walk away from the deal. If you offer prospects the opportunity to pay less if you provide less and they still are unwilling to pay your fee, you need to be willing to tell them, "Thank you, but I don't think this is going to work out."

Revisit Your Value Proposition

You may think your services are valuable, but of course it is more important what your prospects think. If you consistently find that your prospects are unwilling to pay you at the fee level you require and feel is appropriate, it may be time to think about offering a different type of consulting service.

Conclusion

Lowering your fees is a dangerous practice. Instead, target prospects who are willing and able to pay your fees and find ways to deliver more value to your clients. Offer your clients options so they can select the level of value they are willing to fund. If all else fails, be willing to walk away from a negotiation. If this happens consistently, however, seriously reconsider whether your value proposition is strong enough to attract clients.

CHAPTER 22

Chasing Prospects

K EN HABLOW, MY WEBMASTER (www.khgraphics.com), occasionally experiences a common problem that can drive consultants
crazy. His prospects don't return his calls or e-mails.

Here is what typically happens. He receives a phone call from a
small company that wants to create or update a website. He discusses their objectives with them and identifies what they need. Then,
through a series of e-mail conversations, he develops a preliminary
outline of the structure and function of the website. Based on their
response, he submits a proposal that outlines what he will do and
what it will cost. This is often when the conversation stops. The
prospect simply does not respond.

Ken typically e-mails them to ask if they have made a decision,
how their plans are progressing, if they need additional information,
or if there is anything he can do to move things along. Often he
receives no response at all. He is just left wondering whether they
have made a decision, abandoned the project, or selected a different

firm. He typically makes one last attempt to reach the prospect, telling them something like, "If you have changed your plans, it is perfectly okay, but please let me know either way."

Ken has learned over the years that chasing prospects rarely helps the situation. Instead of expending a great deal of energy obsessively worrying about a prospect that has stopped communicating with him, he moves on to the next one. He knows that if prospects are interested, they know how to reach him.

The Challenge

Dealing with nonresponsive prospects is one of the most difficult parts of selling consulting services. Consultants can drive themselves insane worrying about why their prospects aren't getting back to them. Chasing such prospects is generally an exercise in futility. Here are some of the typical thoughts that go through the minds of consultants when their prospects don't respond to them:

◻ *"I thought our conversation went very well. I just don't understand why they won't get back to me."*

◻ *"How many times should I call or send e-mails? I don't want to pester them and I don't want to appear desperate, but they are being rude."*

◻ *"If I call, should I leave a message? If I don't leave a message, will they know through their caller ID that I have called ten times today?"*

◻ *"I am angry. I spent a lot of time speaking with the prospect and putting together a proposal. The least they could do is tell me they have gone in a different direction."*

Here are three basic things you should know about how most prospects deal with salespeople, including consultants:

1. They lie.
2. They often don't tell the whole truth.
3. They lie.

For some reason, fine, upstanding people who never deliberately lie in their personal or business lives feel it is okay to lie to salespeople. They say things like:

- *"We are going to think it over"* ... even though they have already made up their minds.

- *"We definitely want to move forward with this work"* ... even though they are on the fence about it and haven't received the appropriate approvals.

- *"We don't have a budget for this work"* ... even though they actually do.

- *"This is my decision to make"* ... even though there are many others involved in the decision.

- *"We're not talking to other people about this work"* ... when they really are.

- *"We will get back to you next week"* ... even though they have no real plans to do so.

Needless to say, this problem is a major challenge for consultants and a difficult road hazard on the path to establishing and maintaining a successful consulting practice.

Solutions

As a consultant, you need to anticipate unresponsive prospects and take measures that will help you to minimize the chasing, avoid the anxiety, and keep your dignity. Some possible solutions follow.

Establish Mini-Agreements Along the Way with Your Prospects

Try walking your prospects through a series of mini-agreements in which they consent to participate in the specific steps in the process. For instance, if they contact you via telephone and say, "Why don't you send me your literature?" respond by saying, "I would be happy to send you my literature. If I do, will you agree to answer my call next week so that we can discuss whether it makes sense for us to meet?"

If you are meeting with them and they say, "Why don't you put together a proposal?" say something like, "I would be happy to write a proposal that will include a number of options for how we can work together. I will do so if you agree to meet with me next week to discuss it."

If they won't agree to these next steps, then they are likely not serious about working with you. It may be better for you to decline to expend the time and effort of sending the literature or writing the proposal.

Limit How Many Times You Try to Follow Up

Follow up once or twice, perhaps once by e-mail and once by phone a week later. Then just drop it. Prospects will contact you if they are interested in proceeding.

Don't Appear Desperate

If you seem very anxious about securing the work, prospects will have a less positive view of you. It is better to act as if you are independently wealthy and don't need the business.

Don't Make Assumptions

You could easily assume that you have lost the business or that your prospect is just being rude. But there may be a very good reason why prospects have not gotten back to you right away. They or their boss might be on vacation. There might be some pressing issues taking up their attention. Or they may just be slow in making decisions. Unfortunately, you have to work on their timetable. Be patient.

Never Show Anger

After stewing in your office for a week because your prospect hasn't returned your call, you could easily call and leave an angry message. This would be inappropriate and can only hurt your chances of winning the business. Word could also get around in the marketplace and sabotage your chances of winning business with other prospects.

Recognize That You Are Not Going to Win Them All

Even the best consultants, who provide services their prospects desperately need, don't win every piece of business they pursue. There may be some very good reasons why a competitor is a better fit for a particular prospect. Even if the prospect is making a mistake by selecting a different consultant, that's just part of the game. Don't be disillusioned. If a prospect eventually gets back to you and says, "We have gone in a different direction," don't argue or voice your displeasure. Instead, briefly mention your disappointment and wish them well. If they are amenable, you may also want to explore with them why they chose another consultant.

Conclusion

Avoid chasing prospects, one of the many road hazards on the route to becoming a successful consultant. Doing so will drive you crazy and make you appear desperate and unprofessional. Instead, learn how to make mini-agreements during each step of the sales process; limit how many times you follow up; don't appear desperate; and never show your anger. Understand that you are not going to win them all.

PART 5

Getting More Mileage
Out of Your Business

CHAPTER 23

Taking Stock of What's Working and What's Not

AFTER I HAD BEEN IN BUSINESS about seven years, someone asked me four important questions that I could not answer:

1. Are you receiving a sufficient number of leads?
2. Are you receiving the right kinds of leads?
3. How good a job are you doing at converting your leads into new business?
4. How long does it take for you to convert a lead into a new client?

These are important questions. Knowing the answers would allow me to track my progress or failure. I would also be able to take the appropriate corrective action if I found I was receiving too few leads, not receiving the right kinds of leads, or not effectively converting leads into new business.

I decided to start keeping track. Every time I received a lead for any one of my consulting services, whether via telephone, mail, e-mail, or word of mouth, I made an entry in a spreadsheet I call "My Lead Tracker." It contains the following columns:

- Name of prospect
- Date lead was received
- How the lead was generated (i.e., referral, marketing method)
- Type of project
- New prospect or former client
- Industry sector
- Whether or not I was asked to submit a proposal
- Result: Win or loss
- If loss, why
- If win, date of win

After several years I was able to compute the following statistics:

- **Ratio of leads to proposals:** This is the percentage of leads that resulted in a meeting with the prospect. Fifty-five percent of my leads resulted in meetings with prospects, and at every one of these meetings, the prospect asked me to write a proposal. This meant that a little more than half of the leads I was receiving were serious inquiries.
- **Ratio of proposals to sales:** This is the percentage of the proposals I wrote that led to a sale. Forty-one percent of my proposals led to sales. In the majority of cases, I was competing against other consulting firms.
- **Ratio of leads to sales:** This is the percentage of leads that I eventually converted into clients. Twenty-two percent of my leads resulted in new business.

You are probably wondering, as I was: Are these results good or bad? Without comparative data from other consultants, I did not really know. But having this data helped me to better understand my business. For example, each time I received a lead I knew there was about a one in five chance that it would turn into new business. And each time I submitted a proposal, I knew that I had about a 40 percent chance of winning the business. My goal was to try to improve those ratios.

My spreadsheet also enabled me to track:

- How long it took to convert a lead into a sale

◘   Where my leads were coming from

◘   What type of lead I was most successful in converting to a sale

◘   Whether my lead stream was increasing or decreasing

◘   Whether my closure rate was increasing or decreasing

Here are some of the measures many consulting firms use to help them keep track of their business:

◘   **Sales:** The dollar amount each consultant sells to clients.

◘   **Realization:** The dollar amount each consultant actually bills to clients.

◘   **Time:** The amount of time each consultant devotes to: Business development activities, such as marketing, prospect visits, and proposal writing; filing and general administrative work, such as attending internal meetings, billing clients, keeping track of time, and client work.

◘   **Utilization (also called billable time):** The amount of hours each consultant bills to clients as a percentage of the amount of hours the consultant is paid by the firm (typically forty hours). For example, if the consultant bills clients for thirty of the forty hours in the week, the utilization rate is 75 percent. If the consultant bills for fifty hours in the week, the utilization rate is 125 percent.

◘   **Write-Offs:** Often a consultant spends more time on a project than he or she is able to bill to a client. The dollar value of that time (e.g., 20 non-billable hours times $250 per hour billing rate = $5,000) would be written off. Most firms frown on write-offs, preferring that consultants use their time efficiently and charge as much time as possible to their clients.

The Challenge

Any good businessperson needs to keep careful track of what's working well and what is not. This requires that you plan what you are going to measure ahead of time and then maintain ongoing records. Most importantly, you need to use this information to improve your business. For instance:

◻ **If you are spending more time on your projects than you can bill to your client,** become more efficient, delegate tasks to less expensive consultants, or lower your rates.

◻ **If you are busy but still not achieving the income level you desire,** then you need to reduce your expenses, raise your rates, provide higher-value services that can command higher fees, or change your consulting business model.

◻ **If you are not receiving high-quality leads from your direct marketing efforts,** perhaps you should scale back or abandon these efforts.

◻ **If you are receiving high-quality leads from your advertising or involvement in professional networking groups,** perhaps you should devote more resources and time to these activities.

◻ **If you are converting a small percentage of your leads into sales,** you need to gain a better understanding of why this might be the case and perhaps improve your selling skills and proposals, change your pricing, or assess whether your marketing is targeting the appropriate prospects.

◻ **If it is taking you longer and longer from the time you receive a lead to the time you close the deal,** you need to develop sales approaches that will shorten the time it takes you to close sales.

◻ **If your lead stream is declining,** you need to increase your marketing activities.

◻ **If you are not receiving enough leads for one or more of your service lines,** you need to evaluate whether you should devote more attention to marketing that service line or perhaps abandon it altogether.

◻ **If the leads you are receiving are tire-kickers rather than quality leads,** you need to improve your lead-generation strategies.

Solutions

Metrics can help you work on the big picture rather than just in the nitty-gritty details of your consulting business. Use the following three steps to help you keep track of the success and operational efficiency of your business.

Decide Which Metrics Are Important to Track

What measures you use will depend on your business model and which information would be most helpful to you. Take a strategic look at your business and identify the appropriate metrics.

You may or may not feel it is important to track your time the same way large consulting firms do. When I left a large consulting firm to start on my own, I kept careful track of my time using QuickBooks. After several months, I realized two things. First, it was taking me thirty minutes a day or more to track my time. Second, the information wasn't that useful to me. You will need to decide for yourself.

It may be more important for you to track the effectiveness of your various marketing efforts. If so, you will need to develop systems to help you track which marketing efforts are working and which are not.

It may be important for you to track the success of your sales process. If so, you might want to use a strategy something like the one I described above for tracking leads, proposals, and the percentage of leads and proposals that lead to new business.

Develop Systems to Monitor the Metrics

You can keep handwritten records, develop your own spreadsheet programs, or buy commercially available tracking software. Regardless of your choice, you will find that ease of use is more important than bells and whistles.

Evaluate the Results on a Regular Basis

It is important that you schedule time each month, or at least once a quarter, to review the results and develop action plans for making needed changes to aspects such as your marketing activities, proposal writing, fees, and selling process.

Conclusion

You can get more mileage out of your business if you implement systems to take stock of what is working and what is not. Experiment with different metrics to determine which ones are most beneficial to you.

CHAPTER 24

Establishing a Board of Advisers

D AN K ING of Career Planning and Management, Inc. (www.CareerFirm.com) knows the value of taking advice from others. He provides career coaching to business executives. When he founded his business, he formed his own board of advisers to help him grow.

He asked three colleagues to serve on his board. One was a financial planner who looked at things in terms of dollars and cents. Another was an organizational development consultant with a creative, socially minded, humanistic orientation. The third was a good friend who knew Dan's personality and tendency to want to make decisions independently. This person was able to listen to the suggestions from the other two advisers and rephrase them in a way that Dan could easily digest without resistance. The board met informally on a quarterly basis for several years.

Dan felt that his advisers did a great job of helping him to focus and look at his business from a different vantage point. He describes the feedback he received as objective, balanced, and extremely valuable: "It made me get out of my head that I could just figure it all out for myself. Just like men don't ask for directions, we think that we are just supposed to be able to work everything out in our business by ourselves. That's just not possible."

Dan also confided that since he did not pay his board, he initially felt guilty that his advisers were not receiving much in return from him. All he offered them was a meal. But when he shared his concerns with his advisers, they assured him that they learned a lot from each other and enjoyed the giving as much as he enjoyed the receiving.

The Challenge

One of the advantages of working for an organization is that there are colleagues who have a vested interest in your success. They can help you by:

- Providing technical expertise
- Reviewing your work
- Offering advice on how to improve your work
- Suggesting new ideas

When you are on your own, you don't have this type of support roaming the hallways. Instead, you are forced to rely on people you pay, such as your accountant, banker, or attorney, who individually may not have a full understanding of your business. Perhaps you periodically ask for advice from family and friends, who also do not understand your business particularly well or dedicate a great deal of time focusing on the challenges of your business.

Solutions

Independent consultants need to develop creative approaches toward seeking advice about starting and growing their businesses. Most independent consultants end up attempting to perform all the tasks required for their business, everything from strategic planning to emptying the trash. But savvy professionals know:

- They do not have all the answers.

◻ Working day and night, it is easy to become blind to other possibilities about the future of their business.

◻ There are many people who can help them improve their businesses.

Here are two approaches for enlisting the help of others to help you step back and work *on* your business instead of just *in* your business.

Establish a Formal Board of Advisers

There are many methods of establishing some type of advisory group. A formal approach would be similar to a board of directors of a major corporation. The members of the board could meet on a regular basis to discuss your strategic plans, and you would pay them for their participation.

More typically, independent consultants establish a small group of advisers who meet with them on a regular basis without pay to discuss the business. Here is how to get started.

Recruit the advisers. Three to five advisers is the optimal number. These should be people you trust who can bring differing perspectives about your business. They need to be willing to commit time and energy to understand your business and attend meetings. They also need to be good listeners who have the patience to guide you.

Set ground rules. The meetings should have a defined structure that allows meaningful work to be accomplished. Distribute an agenda to the group ahead of time listing clear objectives and start and stop times. I suggest you treat the group to a nice meal, but don't make the meal the main agenda item.

Ask questions. Use the group as a sounding board. Suggest possible new directions you are contemplating and ask them for their thoughts. Share your concerns with them.

Use their advice. It is important that you be open-minded during the meetings. Instead of objecting to suggestions, probe for more information. Most importantly, commit to using at least some of the advice.

Start an Informal Mutual Advisory Group

Back in chapter 19, I mentioned the Enterprise Group. For three years, this group of six senior independent consultants met every two weeks for several hours over dinner to serve as a mutual advisory group. During each meeting we would take turns sharing what was working with our businesses and what was not. Here are a few lessons I learned from this experience.

Recruit noncompeting consultants. It is important that members of the group do not provide the same or even overlapping services. If the services overlap, members might be unwilling to speak frankly about prospects or marketing strategies. Complete openness and honesty is critical.

Limit the size of the group. If you plan to spend two hours together each session, include no more than six members. Otherwise, the time for the group to devote to each person's business will be insufficient.

Make certain everyone's business is discussed at each meeting. Keep the group focused so that there is ample time for everyone to check in and discuss the current state of their business with the group.

Maintain a spirit of openness. It is important that each member feels free to discuss the challenges they are facing with their business. The group just won't be that useful if people are reluctant to share sensitive information about problems or fees.

Make certain group members follow through. Hold each member accountable for using the good suggestions offered by the group. Otherwise, you will all be wasting your time.

Make sure process issues are discussed at each meeting. During each meeting, ask questions such as, "Is this working for you? What went well tonight and what did not? How can we be even more helpful to each other? What lessons have we learned tonight about future meetings?"

Conclusion

Just as CEOs rely on their board of directors for input and advice, a trusted group of advisers will help your business continue to move forward successfully. Formulating a board of advisers or an informal mutual advisory group can help you:

- Navigate the tough times.
- Reduce the blind spots you have about your business.
- Take your business to the next level.

CHAPTER 25

Conducting Research

S EVERAL YEARS AGO, the Northeast Human Resources Association
(NEHRA) distributed a Request for Proposals (RFP) seeking speakers
for their upcoming annual convention. NEHRA is the largest human
resource association in my region. The conference was certain to be
an event that would be well attended by my target market, human
resource professionals. I very much wanted to speak there.

The RFP stated that the theme of the conference was "Staying
Ahead of the Curve." They were looking for speakers who could present on the topic of how senior human resource professionals were
planning for anticipated changes in their organizations during the
next few years.

Although I had done a lot of work for human resource depart-
ments in many organizations, I was not an expert on how human
resource professionals should prepare for the future. I thought that I
would just have to wait until next year's convention.

I was just about ready to delete the RFP from my in-box when I
came up with a brainstorm. I could offer to conduct a survey of sen-

ior human resource professionals on this topic and then present the results at the convention. That way, I would use my survey expertise to gather and summarize information provided to me by active senior human resource professionals.

My plan had another important benefit. I knew that if I informed the people I interviewed that the results of the study would be presented at the annual convention, there was a good chance they would consent to participate. That would give me the opportunity to have meaningful conversations with many of the senior-most human resource professionals in the region—my most important group of potential prospects.

I wrote a proposal and sent it to the program committee. They received proposals from hundreds of interested speakers and selected me to be one of the presenters. I had met their selection criteria perfectly. Even though I wasn't an expert on the convention's stated theme, I would be presenting something they wanted the conference attendees to hear.

The Challenge

Independent consultants often face the dilemma of wanting to be viewed as an authority on a particular topic even when they have not conducted much work in that area and have never spoken or written about it. Here are three scenarios when this might be the case:

1. You are just beginning your consulting business and need to do everything possible to establish your credibility. Without a client list, testimonials from satisfied clients, and a track record in the field, it is difficult to be known as the consulting expert in any particular field.

2. You are a seasoned consultant seeking to expand your business by launching a new service line. You need to establish your credibility in this new area.

3. You want to consult in a new cutting-edge field. There is a problem that you believe you can solve for clients, even though, as far as you know, nobody has consulted in this area before. You want to establish yourself as the expert before anyone else enters this niche.

Solutions

Conducting a research study, which can make you an instant expert, can be the solution in all of these scenarios.

You can use a variety of methods to conduct the study, including a mail- or Web-based survey, an interview study, or a macroanalysis of published articles on the topic. Once you have conducted the study, you will be in possession of the most current information on the topic. You will instantly become the go-to expert, with the wherewithal to deliver speeches, write press releases and articles, and conduct radio and television interviews. Most importantly, this newfound expertise can put you on the fast track for landing new business.

A step-by-step procedure for conducting a research study follows.

Formulate the Preliminary Research Design

Your preliminary research design should address a few basic questions:

- How will this research benefit my consulting business?
- What key issues will the study explore?
- What methodology will I use (e.g., Web survey, mail survey, telephone interviews, in-person interviews, etc.)?
- Who will need to participate in the study (e.g., types of organizations, job titles, geographical location)?
- How will this study enable me to make meaningful contact with potential prospects?
- How will the study benefit the participants?

Find a Sponsor

Pitch the idea to a reputable professional association, newspaper, magazine, radio station, television station, or website whose members, readers, or listeners are in your target market. Tell the executive directors, editors, or producers that you are planning on conducting a research study that will be of interest to their constituents. Ask them if they are interested in publishing the results or having you present the results at an upcoming meeting or conference.

A sponsor can lend credibility to the study, which in turn will help you recruit participants. Sponsorship will also help you to widely disseminate the results once the study has been completed. A sponsor that really likes the idea might even offer to help you collect the data or share some of the expenses.

Develop the Questions

You will then need to develop the appropriate set of questions to ask participants. Think about the end at the beginning. In other words, make certain that the questions you ask will enable you to write a report or present a speech that will contain valuable information and position you as the expert.

It is important, of course, to ask all participants an identical set of questions. If you are going to conduct an interview study, you probably want to limit the interview to no more than thirty minutes. If you are going to conduct a survey, try to include no more than thirty questions.

If you are not sure about the right questions to ask, consider conducting several open-ended interviews with potential participants to discuss the topic. This should give you a better idea of what topics to include and what types of questions participants will be able to answer.

Recruit Participants

Finding people to participate in the study can be a challenge. Ideally, your sponsor will be able to provide you with a list of people to contact. Alternatively, you may have to develop your own list. Here is a three-step strategy I have used to recruit participants for a telephone interview study:

1. **Initial correspondence:** Send an initial letter to the prospective participants describing the purpose of the study, the sponsor, the length of the interview, and the benefits of participating. Offer participants a special detailed executive summary of the results that will be available only to participants. Tell them that you will call them to set up a time for the interview. Ask them to alert their executive assistant that you will be calling.
2. **Follow-up telephone call:** Call to schedule the interview.
3. **Conduct the interview.**

Prepare an Executive Summary

After you have collected and analyzed the data, prepare an executive summary report. It should include your insights and recommendations, as well as the data. Send it to each of the participants, as promised.

Meet with Participants

If the study involved interviewing potential prospects for your services, offer to meet with each of them individually to discuss the results. Since these are your potential prospects, this will be of additional value to them and could prove to be very valuable to you.

Provide the Report or Speech to the Sponsor

Follow through with your commitment to your sponsor by writing an article for their publication, delivering a speech at one of their meetings, or participating in a radio or television show.

Distribute the Results Widely

While the data is still timely, it is important for you to leverage it in as many ways as possible. Consider sending press releases about the results to the relevant media outlets, writing papers for other publications in the field, delivering speeches to other professional groups, and offering the executive summary for free on your website or via a direct mail campaign.

Conclusion

You can get more mileage out of your business by conducting timely research studies. Although it requires considerable planning and effort, research can pay huge dividends. Whether you are just starting out, an experienced consultant interested in launching a new service line, or someone looking to become the expert in a brand-new consulting arena, such a study can quickly position you as the expert in the field. It can also put you in direct contact with potential clients.

CHAPTER 26

Maintaining Readiness to Adapt to Change

A RITE AID DRUGSTORE recently moved to my town, which made me think of my father's drugstore business thirty years ago.

My father was a pharmacist. He owned and operated different drugstores for more than twenty-five years, the last one located in a small suburban neighborhood. His customers called him "Doc." They counted on him for health-related advice and counsel. He really cared about them, knew most of them by name, and provided personalized services, such as home delivery and charge accounts.

Business was good until a Rite Aid moved in just a few blocks away. While Rite Aid did not offer the same level of service and did not get to know their customers on a personal basis, they *were* less expensive.

The writing was on the wall, but my father felt helpless to do anything about it. Operating a drugstore was all he knew. Much of his life savings were invested in the store. He couldn't just relocate and if he did, he would probably face the same situation.

Over the course of several years his business steadily declined, and he eventually had to close his doors. He suffered the fate common to many in business both then and today. He failed to find a way to adapt to the changing realities of the marketplace.

The Challenge

There is only one thing for certain in the business world—things are changing and will continue to change. Examples of the many types of changes that can rapidly lead to failure for your consulting business include:

- **Technological changes:** digitizing of content, businesses moving to the Web
- **Changes in the competitive landscape:** outsourcing to third world countries with less expensive labor costs
- **Geopolitical changes:** changes in trade regulations, the changing value of the dollar, international embargos, wars
- **Changes in customer preferences:** generational differences, aging of the population, desire to "do it ourselves" rather than hire consultants

All organizations, ranging from solo practitioners and small-business owners to huge multinational corporations, are vulnerable to these changes. Think that rapid change can't crush *your* consulting business? What would happen to your business if:

- A college student figured out a way to conduct your business on the Web?
- The government regulations that drive your business were dramatically changed?
- A competitor was able to provide essentially the same services twice as fast at half the cost?
- The value of the dollar decreased by 50 percent?

These types of changes are happening every day and will continue at an increasingly faster rate. Yet consultants typically conduct business as though their business environment will always remain stable. They do this at their own peril.

Solutions

If you want your consulting business to survive long term, you can't be complacent. Instead of being a late adopter, you need to be the early adopter. Anticipate changes in the needs of your prospects and continually develop new services that will address these needs.

Constantly Scan Your Environment

Bill Gates is known to lock himself up for a week each year to immerse himself in reports about other industries, trends, and environmental events that might impact Microsoft. You need to evaluate changes in your external environment as well, along with the potential impact of those changes on your business.

Discern Your Core Identity

It is important for you to balance change with staying true to who you are. If you try to adapt to changes by making radical changes in your services that are inconsistent with your values and mission, you are doomed to fail. For example, if your passion and focus is helping individuals through the emotional turmoil of career transition, it may not make sense for you to switch gears and help organizations open up new manufacturing facilities.

Maintain a Readiness to Change

You must be poised to constantly change. As an independent consultant, you need to maintain strategic agility. As needs in the marketplace change, quickly take note of those changes and develop new and different services that address the current needs of your prospects. Keep up with the literature in your field, as well as the literature in related fields. Attend speeches by thought leaders in your area of expertise. Tune in to the long-term plans of your clients and other organizations in your niche. Then prepare "what-if" scenarios to plan what you will do if the anticipated changes actually happen.

Conclusion

Nothing stays the same. Businesses that don't evolve in response to changes in the marketplace will eventually die. The successful consulting business you establish today may not be viable two years from today because of these changes. If you want your business to weather difficult economic times, changes in technology, and changes in the needs of your prospects, you need to be like a chameleon, able to change as your environment changes.

You must be proactive. Start by systematically scanning your environment for changes that are likely to impact your business, discern and stay true to your core identity, and maintain a constant readiness to change.

Conclusion

F YOU HAVE MADE IT this far into the book, you are no doubt committed to consulting. By now you know that to be a successful independent consultant, you will have to develop a niche, be smart and diligent about marketing your services, provide value to your clients, and learn how to network.

You have also learned that consulting is not for everyone. After all, you might not enjoy being a slave to the corporate beast, where your boss tells you where to be, when to be there, and what to do. As a consultant, you can break those shackles of slavery. But are you willing to pay the price for freedom? Are you willing to exit your comfort zone? If you have been working nine to five for many years, you have probably grown accustomed to having your nights and weekends off, four weeks of annual vacation, health benefits, and a regular monthly paycheck. Life will be very different as an independent consultant. You will be able to set your own work hours, but you will likely work many more hours than you did as an employee. You might be lonely. You will need to purchase your own benefits and keep your own books. Striking out on your own is not for everyone. You need to be fully committed and have a passion for self-employment. It's like the difference between the bacon and eggs on your breakfast plate. The chicken was not fully committed, but the pig was. You need to be like the pig.

If you *do* have the passion, however, being an independent consultant is a wonderful life. Each project is a challenge; each day is something different. The rewards, both financial and lifestyle, are determined mostly by your own drive and enthusiasm.

So how do you know if you have succeeded in implementing the strategies described in these pages? How do you know if you have arrived as an independent consultant or remain a wannabe? Sure, you can look at your net income, but that often doesn't tell the whole story. Here are seven rites of passage you can use to determine whether you have arrived:

1. You turn down an offer for a full-time job. Until you face this acid test, you will not truly understand the depth of your commitment. And without full commitment to self-employment, your business will likely not succeed.

2. You develop a niche. Beginning consultants often flounder because they are unclear as to exactly what service they provide and for whom they provide it.

3. You sell beyond your immediate circle. Successful consultants know how to proactively generate business outside of their immediate contacts.

4. You say "no" to a prospect. You must be able to turn down business because it does not fit your expertise, fee structure, or business model.

5. You invest in your business. A new computer, new telephones, a website, and a marketing brochure all require investments of time and money. Until you are willing to invest in your own business, you're not really serious about your consulting practice.

6. You increase your fees. Experienced consultants have proven to themselves and to others that they provide value. They feel justified and comfortable raising their fees.

7. You weather a dry spell. It is inevitable that your consulting business will encounter ups and downs. Successful businesses are able to persist during the downturns. This may mean increasing your marketing activities, digging into your savings, or fine-tuning your services to meet the changing needs of the marketplace.

If you are like most independent consultants I know, once you have achieved a little success, traversed through the seven rites of passage, and tasted the freedom that comes with the profession, you will never again want to don the shackles of working for someone else.

Good luck, and may the spirit and benefits of entrepreneurship always be with you.

Recommended Reading

Block, P. *Flawless Consulting: A Guide to Getting Your Expertise Used.* San Diego, CA: Pfeiffer & Company, 1981.

Cohen, W. A. *How to Make it Big as a Consultant.* New York: AMACOM, 1984.

Connor, R. A. and Davidson, J. P. *Marketing Your Consulting and Professional Services.* New York: John Wiley & Sons, Inc., 1985.

Falkenstien, L. *Nichecraft: Using Your Business to Focus Your Business, Corner Your Market, and Make Customers Seek You Out.* Portland, OR: Niche Press, 2000.

Gerber, M. E. *The E-Myth Revisited: Why Most Small Businesses Don't Work and What to Do About It.* New York: Harper-Collins Books, 1995.

Greiner, L. E. and Metzger, R. O. *Consulting to Management.* Englewood Cliffs, NJ: Prentice-Hall, Inc., 1983.

Harding, F. *Rain Making: The Professional's Guide to Attracting New Clients.* Holbrook, MA: Bob Adams, Inc., 1994.

Hayden, C. J. *Get Clients Now!™: A 28-Day Marketing Program for Professionals and Consultants.* New York: AMACOM, 1999.

Kremmer, J. *1001 Ways to Market Your Books, 6th Edition.* Fairfield, IA: Open Horizons, 2006.

Lawler, E. L. and Worley, C. G. *Built to Change: How to Achieve Sustained Organizational Effectiveness.* San Francisco, CA: Jossey-Bass, 2006.

Levinson, J. C. *Guerrilla Marketing: Secrets for Making Big Profits from Your Small Business.* Boston, MA: Houghton Mifflin Company, 1993.

Linneman, R. E. and Stanton, J. L. *Making Niche Marketing Work: How to Grow Bigger By Acting Smaller.* New York: McGraw-Hill, Inc., 1991.

Lizotte, K. *The Expert's Edge.* New York: McGraw-Hill, Inc., 1991.

Parinello, A. *Selling to VITO, 2nd Edition.* Holbrook, MA: Adams Media Corporation, 1999.

Reiss, F. *The Publishing Game: Publish a Book in 30 Days.* Boston, MA: Peanut Butter and Jelly Press, 2003.

Sandler, D. H. with Hayes, J. *You Can't Teach a Kid to Ride a Bike at a Seminar: The Sandler Sales Institute's 7-Step System for Successful Selling.* New York: Penguin Books, 1995.

Tepper, R. *Become a Top Consultant: How the Experts Do It.* New York: John Wiley & Sons, 1985.

Weiss, A. *Million Dollar Consulting: The Professional's Guide to Growing a Practice.* New York: McGraw-Hill, Inc., 1992.

Weiss, A. *Money Talks: How to Make a Million as a Speaker.* New York: McGraw-Hill, Inc., 1998.

Williams, B. *In Business for Yourself.* Lanham, MD: Scarborough House Publishers, 1993.

Index

About the Authors

Bruce L. Katcher, Ph.D., offers training and mentoring to aspiring and experienced independent consultants (learn more at www.CenterForIndependentConsulting.com). An industrial/organizational psychologist, he is the founder and president of The Discovery Consulting Group, Inc., a management consulting firm based in Sharon, Massachusetts. The firm focuses on employee engagement and retention and conducts employee opinion and customer satisfaction surveys. Among his more than one hundred clients are Alcoa, Delta Dental Plan, Dunkin' Donuts, Johnson & Johnson, the Mayo Clinic, Revlon, Sodexo, the Tata Group, Textron Systems, Timberland, and W. R. Grace. Sign up for his free e-newsletter, *Improving the Workplace*, at www.DiscoveryConsultingGroup.com. His award-winning first book is titled: *30 Reasons Employees Hate Their Managers: What Your People May Be Thinking and What You Can Do About It.*

Adam Snyder is a freelance business writer based in New York. He has been published in dozens of national publications and has ghosted and written numerous business books. Adam is also president of the animation and video company, Rembrandt Films. For more information, visit www.rembrandtfilms.com.